Discrete-Time
Neural Obervers

Discrete-Time Neural Obervers

Analysis and Applications

Alma Y. Alanis

Research Professor, University of Guadalajara, Mexico

Edgar N. Sanchez

Research Professor, CINVESTAV, University of Guadalajara, Mexico

AMSTERDAM • BOSTON • HEIDELBERG • LONDON
NEW YORK • OXFORD • PARIS • SAN DIEGO
SAN FRANCISCO • SINGAPORE • SYDNEY • TOKYO

Academic Press is an imprint of Elsevier

Academic Press is an imprint of Elsevier
125 London Wall, London EC2Y 5AS, United Kingdom
525 B Street, Suite 1800, San Diego, CA 92101-4495, United States
50 Hampshire Street, 5th Floor, Cambridge, MA 02139, United States
The Boulevard, Langford Lane, Kidlington, Oxford OX5 1GB, United Kingdom

Library of Congress Cataloging-in-Publication Data
A catalog record for this book is available from the Library of Congress

British Library Cataloguing-in-Publication Data
A catalogue record for this book is available from the British Library

ISBN: 978-0-12-810543-6

For information on all Academic Press publications
visit our website at https://www.elsevier.com

Working together
to grow libraries in
developing countries

www.elsevier.com • www.bookaid.org

Publisher: Joe Hayton
Acquisition Editor: Chris Katsaropoulos
Editorial Project Manager: Anna Valutkevich
Production Project Manager: Priya Kumaraguruparan
Designer: Maria Inês Cruz

Typeset by VTeX

To our Families.

Contents

About the Authors

Alma Y. Alanis

Alma Y. Alanis was born in Durango, Durango, Mexico, in 1980. She received the BSc degree from Instituto Tecnologico de Durango (ITD), Durango Campus, Durango, Durango, in 2002, the MSc and PhD degrees in electrical engineering from the Advanced Studies and Research Center of the National Polytechnic Institute (CINVESTAV-IPN), Guadalajara Campus, Mexico, in 2004 and 2007, respectively. Since 2008 she has been with University of Guadalajara, where she is currently a Chair Professor in the Department of Computer Science. She is also a member of the Mexican National Research System (SNI-2). She has published papers in recognized international journals and conferences, as well as two international books. Alma Y. Alanis is a Senior Member of the IEEE and Subject and Associated Editor of the Journal of Franklin Institute (Elsevier) and Intelligent Automation & Soft Computing (Taylor & Francis); moreover, she is currently serving as a number of IEEE and IFAC Conference Organizing Committees. In 2013, she received the grant for women in science by L'Oreal-UNESCO-AMC-CONACYT-CONALMEX. In 2015, she received the Research Award Marcos Moshinsky. Since 2008 Alma Y. Alanis is member for the Accredited Assessors record RCEA-CONACYT, evaluating a wide range of national research projects; she has also worked on important project evaluation committees of national and international research projects. Her research interest centers on neural control, backstepping control, block control, and their applications to electrical machines, power systems, and robotics.

Edgar N. Sanchez

Edgar N. Sanchez was born in 1949, in Sardinata, Colombia, South America. He obtained the BSEE, major in Power Systems from Universidad Industrial de Santander (UIS), Bucaramanga, Colombia in 1971, the MSEE from CINVESTAV-IPN (Advanced Studies and Research Center of the National Polytechnic Institute), major in Automatic Control, Mexico City, Mexico, in 1974, and the Docteur Ingenieur degree in Automatic Control from Institut Nationale Polytechnique de Grenoble, France, in 1980.

In 1971, 1972, 1975, and 1976, Edgar N. Sanchez worked for different Electrical Engineering consulting companies in Bogota, Colombia. In 1974, he became professor of Electrical Engineering Department of UIS, Colombia. From January 1981 to November 1990, he worked as a researcher at the Electrical Research Institute, Cuernavaca, Mexico. Edgar N. Sanchez was a professor of the graduate program in Electrical Engineering of the Universidad Autonoma de Nuevo Leon (UANL), Monterrey, Mexico, from December 1990 to December 1996. Since January 1997, he has been with CINVESTAV-IPN, Guadalajara Campus, Mexico, as a Professor of Electrical Engineering graduate programs. His research interest center on Neural Networks and Fuzzy Logic as applied to Automatic Control systems. He has been the advisor of 21 PhD theses and 40 MSc theses.

He was granted the USA National Research Council Award as a research associate at NASA Langley Research Center, Hampton, Virginia, USA (January 1985 to March 1987). He is also a member of the Mexican National Research System (promoted to highest rank, III, in 2005), the Mexican Academy of Science, and the Mexican Academy of Engineering. Edgar N. Sanchez has published 4 books, more than 150 technical papers in international journals and conferences, and has served as a reviewer for different international journals and conferences. He has also been a member of many international conferences, IPCs, organized both by IEEE and IFAC.

Acknowledgment

The authors thank CONACYT (its Spanish acronym stands for National Council of Sciences and Technology), Mexico, for financial support on projects CB-256769 and CB-257200. They also thank CUCEI-UDG (its Spanish acronym stands for University Center of Exact Sciences and Engineering of the University of Guadalajara), Mexico and CINVESTAV-IPN (its Spanish acronym stands for Advanced Studies and Research Center of the National Polytechnic Institute), Mexico, for the provided support to write this book. The first author also thanks the support of "Fundacion Marcos Moshinsky".

In addition, they thank Alexander G. Loukianov (CINVESTAV, Guadalajara), Carlos Lopez-Franco (CUCEI, UDG), Diana A. Urrego (MSc, former student at CINVESTAV, Unidad Guadalajara), Esteban Hernandez-Vargas (MSc, former student at CINVESTAV, Unidad Guadalajara), Jordany Jauregui (CUCEI, UDG), Jorge D. Rios (CUCEI, UDG), Gustavo Hernandez-Mejia (CUCEI, UDG), Nancy Arana-Daniel (CUCEI, UDG), Salvador Carlos-Hernandez (CINVESTAV, Saltillo) who have contributed in different ways to this book.

CHAPTER 1

Introduction

ABSTRACT

This chapter presents an introduction which includes motivation, objectives, problem statement, book structure, and notation. All this information is necessary to have an overview of the themes contained in the book.

KEYWORDS

Neural observers	Motivation	Problem statement
State-of-the-art		

CONTENTS

1.1 INTRODUCTION

Modern control systems usually require very structured knowledge about the system to be controlled; such knowledge should be represented in terms of differential or difference equations. This mathematical description of the dynamic system is named the model. There can be several motives for establishing mathematical descriptions of dynamic systems, such as simulation, prediction, fault detection, and control system design.

There are two ways to obtain a model: it can be derived in a deductive manner using physics laws, or it can be inferred from a set of data collected during a practical experiment:

- The first method can be simple, but in many cases it is excessively time-consuming; it would be unrealistic or impossible to obtain an accurate model in this way.
- The second method, which is commonly referred to as system identification, could be a useful shortcut for deriving mathematical models.

Although system identification not always results in an accurate model, a satisfactory model can be often obtained with reasonable efforts. The main drawback is the requirement to conduct a practical experiment, which brings the system through its range of operation [4,21].

Discrete-Time Neural Observers. DOI:10.1016/B978-0-12-810543-6.00001-0

Many of the nonlinear control publications assume complete accessibility of the system state; this is not always possible. For this reason, nonlinear state estimation is a very important topic for nonlinear control [24]. State estimation has been studied by many authors who have obtained interesting results in different directions. Most of those results need the use of a special nonlinear transformation [20] or a linearization technique [7,12]. Such approaches can be considered as a relatively simple method to construct nonlinear observers; however, they do not consider uncertainties [16,17,27]. In practice, there exist external and internal uncertainties. Observers which have good performance even in the presence of model and disturbance uncertainties are called robust; their design process is too complex [1–3,9,26]. All the approaches mentioned above need previous knowledge of the plant model, at least partially. Recently, other kinds of observer have emerged for unknown plant dynamics; they are named neural observers [11,13,18,22,24,25].

Neural networks have grown to be a well-established methodology, which allows solving very difficult problems in engineering, as exemplified by their applications to identification and control of general nonlinear and complex systems. In particular, the use of recurrent neural networks for modeling and learning has rapidly increased in recent years [6,10,14,15,19,25].

There exist different training algorithms for neural networks, which, however, normally encounter some technical problems such as local minima, slow learning, and high sensitivity to initial conditions, among others. As a viable alternative, new training algorithms, e.g., those based on Kalman filtering, have been proposed [5,7,8,28]. Due to the fact that training of a neural network typically results in a nonlinear problem, the Extended Kalman Filter (EKF) is a common tool to use instead of a linear Kalman filter [8].

As is well known [23,25], recurrent high order neural networks (RHONN) offer many advantages for modeling of complex nonlinear systems. On the other hand, EKF training for neural networks allows reducing the epoch size and the number of required neurons [8]. Considering these two facts, we propose the use of the EKF training for RHONN in order to model complex nonlinear systems.

The best well-known training approach for recurrent neural networks (RNN) is the back propagation through time learning [28]. However, it is a first order gradient descent method and hence its learning speed could be very slow [28]. Recently, EKF based algorithms have been introduced to train neural networks in order to improve the learning convergence [28]. The EKF training of neural networks, both feedforward and recurrent, has proven to be reliable and practical for many applications over the past ten years [28].

In this book, a recurrent high order neural network (RHONN) is used to design an adaptive recurrent neural observer for nonlinear systems whose mathematical model is assumed to be unknown. The learning algorithm for the RHONN is implemented using an EKF. The respective stability analysis, based on the Lyapunov approach, is included. The applicability of the proposed scheme is illustrated via simulation results for different kinds of MIMO discrete-time nonlinear system, as well as Rotatory Induction Motor, Linear Induction Motor and DC Motor, waste water treatment plant, and the HIV.

1.2 MOTIVATION

For many nonlinear control designs, it is usually assumed that all the system states are measurable. In practice, however, only parts of these states are measured directly. Due to this fact, nonlinear state estimation remains an important topic of study in the nonlinear system theory. For continuous time, recurrent neural observers have also been proposed, and they do not require a precise plant model. Nevertheless, the discrete-time case has not been dealt with the same intensity; thus is a field plentiful of opportunities for research and applications.

Therefore, the major motivation for this book is to develop alternative methodologies to allow the design of robust observers for discrete-time nonlinear systems with unknown dynamics.

1.3 OBJECTIVES

The main objectives of this work are stated as follows:

- To synthesize a full order neural observer for a class of MIMO discrete-time nonlinear systems, using a Recurrent High Order Neural Network trained online with an algorithm based on an EKF.
- To develop a reduced order neural observer for a class of MIMO discrete-time nonlinear systems, using a Recurrent High Order Neural Network trained online with an algorithm based on an EKF.
- To establish stability analyses, using the Lyapunov approach, for each proposed scheme.
- To implement the real time experiments for each proposed scheme.

1.4 PROBLEM STATEMENT

As mentioned above, in modern control systems, complete access to state measurements is often required due to different reasons, e.g.,

- It is not always possible to have the required sensors.
- Sensors are not reliable.
- Sensors have a lot of noise.
- There are no sensors to acquire the required signals.
- Sensors are very expensive.

For many years scientists working on control systems solved this problem (signal without measurement) with observers. Nevertheless, as mentioned above, most of such observers require an accurate mathematical model.

In order to deal with both problems in this book, we propose the use of an RHONN, trained with an EKF algorithm, to design neural observers that can estimate the state variables' measurements completely for all the states or only for a few variables (they will be named full and reduced order neural observers, respectively) with linear and nonlinear output equations and with and without the presence of time-delays. These neural observer schemes are designed in this book including meaningful applications for both real time implementations and academic examples.

1.5   BOOK STRUCTURE

This book presents recent advances in the theory of neural state estimation for discrete-time unknown nonlinear systems with multiple inputs and multiple outputs. The results which appear in the book include rigorous mathematical analyses, based on the Lyapunov approach, to guarantee their properties; in addition, simulation results are included to verify the performance of the corresponding proposed schemes. In order to complete the explanation of these schemes, the final chapter presents experimental results related to their application to an electric three-phase induction motor and to an anaerobic process. These experimental results illustrate the applicability of such proposed schemes, which could also be employed for different applications beyond those presented in this book.

This book is organized as follows:

In *Chapter 2*, mathematical preliminaries are introduced, including stability definitions and the extended Kalman filter training algorithm.

In *Chapter 3*, foundations of a full order neural observer are presented. The proposed scheme is based on an RHONN trained with an online EKF-based algorithm in the presence of disturbances and without time delays. This chapter also includes meaningful applications for real-time state estimation of electromechanical and biological systems. This observer is developed for both scenarios, when the system to be observed has linear or nonlinear outputs.

Chapter 4 presents the reduced order neural observers for discrete-time nonlinear systems with linear or nonlinear outputs. The applicability of this observer is shown with real-time implementations for electromechanical and biological systems.

Chapter 5 includes the extension of the full and reduced order neural observers for discrete-time nonlinear systems in the presence of unknown time delays.

The designed observers are applied for a van der Pol system and for electromechanical systems.

Finally, relevant conclusions and future trends are stated in *Chapter 6*.

1.6   NOTATION

Through this book, we use the following notation:

$k \in \{0\} \cup \mathbb{Z}^+$	Sampling step
$|\bullet|$	Absolute value
$\|\bullet\|$	Euclidean norm for vectors and any adequate norm for matrices
$S(\bullet)$	Sigmoid function
$x \in \Re^n$	Plant state
$\widehat{x} \in \Re^n$	Neural network state
$w_i \in \Re^L$	ith neural network estimated weight vector
$w_i^* \in \Re^L$	ith neural network ideal weight vector
$L_i \in \Re$	Number of high order connections
$u \in \Re^m$	Control action
$\varrho \in \Re^m$	Neural network external input
$z_i \in \Re^{L_i}$	High-order terms
$K \in \Re^{L_i \times m}$	Kalman gain matrix
$P \in \Re^{L_i \times L_i}$	Associated prediction error covariance matrix
$Q \in \Re^{L_i \times L_i}$	Associated state noise covariance matrix
$R \in \Re^{m \times m}$	Associated measurement noise covariance matrix
$g_i \in \Re$	ith neural observer gain
$e \in \Re^p$	Output error
$\widetilde{x} \in \Re^n$	State observer error
$\widetilde{w}_i \in \Re^{L_i}$	Weights estimation error
$l \in \Re^n, l(k) \in \Re^n, l \in \Re^n, l_i \in \Re, l_i(k) \in \Re$	Unknown time delay
$d(k) \in \Re^n, d_i(k) \in \Re$	Unknown disturbances

REFERENCES

[1] F. Chen, M.W. Dunnigan, Comparative study of a sliding-mode observer and Kalman filters for full state estimation in an induction machine, IEE Proceedings – Electric Power Applications 149 (1) (Jan. 2002) 53–64.

[2] F. Chen, H. Khalil, Adaptive control of a class of nonlinear discrete-time systems using neural networks, IEEE Transactions on Automatic Control 40 (5) (1995) 791–801.

[3] D.F. Coutinho, L.P.F.A. Pereira, A robust Luenberger-like observer for induction machines, in: Proceedings IEEE IECON 2005, Nov. 2005.

[4] J.A. Farrell, M.M. Polycarpou, Adaptive Approximation Based Control: Unifying Neural, Fuzzy and Traditional Adaptive Approximation Approaches, John Wiley and Sons, NY, USA, 2006.

[5] L.A. Feldkamp, D.V. Prokhorov, T.M. Feldkamp, Simple and conditioned adaptive behavior from Kalman filter trained recurrent networks, Neural Networks 16 (2003) 683–689.

[6] S.S. Ge, J. Zhang, T.H. Lee, Adaptive neural network control for a class of MIMO nonlinear systems with disturbances in discrete-time, IEEE Transactions on Systems, Man and Cybernetics, Part B 34 (4) (Aug. 2004).

[7] R. Grover, P.Y.C. Hwang, Introduction to Random Signals and Applied Kalman Filtering, 2nd ed., John Wiley and Sons, NY, USA, 1992.

[8] S. Haykin, Kalman Filtering and Neural Networks, John Wiley and Sons, NY, USA, 2001.

[9] H. Huang, G. Feng, J. Cao, Robust state estimation for uncertain neural networks with time-varying delay, IEEE Transactions on Neural Networks 19 (8) (2008) 1329–1339.

[10] S. Jagannathan, Control of a class of nonlinear discrete-time systems using multilayer neural networks, IEEE Transactions on Neural Networks 12 (5) (2001) 1113–1120.

[11] Y.H. Kim, F.L. Lewis, High-Level Feedback Control with Neural Networks, World Scientific, Singapore, 1998.

[12] A.J. Krener, A. Isidori, Linearization by output injection and nonlinear observers, Systems & Control Letters 3 (1983) 47–52.

[13] A.U. Levin, K.S. Narendra, Control of nonlinear dynamical systems using neural networks – part II: observability, identification and control, IEEE Transactions on Neural Networks 7 (1) (Jan. 1996) 30–42.

[14] F.L. Lewis, J. Campos, R. Selmic, Neuro-Fuzzy Control of Industrial Systems with Actuator Nonlinearities, Society of Industrial and Applied Mathematics Press, Philadelphia, 2002.

[15] F.L. Lewis, S. Jagannathan, A. Yesildirek, Neural Network Control of Robot Manipulators and Nonlinear Systems, Taylor and Francis, London, 1999.

[16] J. Li, Y. Zhong, Comparison of three Kalman filters for speed estimation of induction machines, in: Proceedings Industry Applications Conference 2005, Oct. 2005.

[17] Y. Liu, Z. Wang, X. Liu, Design of exponential state estimators for neural networks with mixed time delays, Physics Letters A 364 (5) (May 2007) 401–412.

[18] R. Marino, Observers for single output nonlinear systems, IEEE Transactions on Automatic Control 35 (Sept. 1990) 1054–1058.

[19] K.S. Narendra, K. Parthasarathy, Identification and control of dynamical systems using neural networks, IEEE Transactions on Neural Networks 1 (Mar. 1990) 4–27.

[20] S. Nicosia, A. Tornambe, High-gain observers in the state and parameter estimation of robots having elastic joins, Systems & Control Letters 13 (1989) 331–337.

[21] M. Norgaard, O. Ravn, N.K. Poulsen, L.K. Hansen, Neural Networks for Modelling and Control of Dynamic Systems, Springer-Verlag, New York, USA, 2000.

[22] A.S. Poznyak, E.N. Sanchez, W. Yu, Differential Neural Networks for Robust Nonlinear Control, World Scientific, Singapore, 2001.

[23] G.A. Rovithakis, M.A. Chistodoulou, Adaptive Control with Recurrent High-Order Neural Networks, Springer-Verlag, Berlin, Germany, 2000.

[24] E.N. Sanchez, A.Y. Alanis, G. Chen, Recurrent neural networks trained with Kalman filtering for discrete chaos reconstruction, Dynamics of Continuous, Discrete & Impulsive Systems, Series B 13 (2006) 1–18.

[25] E.N. Sanchez, L.J. Ricalde, Trajectory tracking via adaptive recurrent neural control with input saturation, in: Proceedings of International Joint Conference on Neural Networks'03, Portland, Oregon, USA, July 2003.

[26] B.L. Walcott, S.H. Zak, State observation of nonlinear uncertain dynamical system, IEEE Transactions on Automatic Control 32 (1987) 166–170.

[27] Z. Wang, D.W.C. Ho, X. Liu, State estimation for delayed neural networks, IEEE Transactions on Neural Networks 16 (1) (Jan. 2005) 279–284.

[28] S. Singhal, L. Wu, Training multilayer perceptrons with the extended Kalman algorithm, in: D.S. Touretzky (Ed.), Advances in Neural Information Processing Systems, vol. 1, Morgan Kaufmann, San Mateo, CA, USA, 1989, pp. 133–140.

Mathematical Preliminaries

ABSTRACT

In this chapter, important mathematical preliminaries, which are required for future chapters, are presented. Also the RHONN model is defined, including the EKF-based training algorithm.

KEYWORDS

Discrete-time nonlinear systems

Artificial neural networks

Recurrent high-order neural networks

Extended Kalman filter learning

Discrete-time nonlinear observers

CONTENTS

2.1 STABILITY DEFINITIONS

This section follows [7] closely. Through this book, we use k as the sampling step, $k \in 0 \cup \mathbb{Z}^+$, $|\bullet|$ as the absolute value, and $\|\bullet\|$ as the Euclidean norm for vectors and as any adequate norm for matrices. Consider a Multiple Input Multiple Output (MIMO) nonlinear system:

$$x(k+1) = F(x(k), u(k)), \tag{2.1}$$
$$y(k) = h(x(k)) \tag{2.2}$$

where $x \in \mathfrak{R}^n$, $u \in \mathfrak{R}^m$, and $F \in \mathfrak{R}^n \times \mathfrak{R}^m \to \mathfrak{R}^n$ is a nonlinear function. A schematic representation of this system is included in Fig. 2.1.

Definition 2.1 ([10]). System (2.1)–(2.2) is said to be forced, or to have inputs. In contrast, a system described by an equation without explicit presence of an input u,

$$x(k+1) = F(x(k)), \tag{2.3}$$

is said to be unforced. It can be obtained after selecting the input u as a feedback function of the state

$$u(k) = \xi(x(k)). \tag{2.4}$$

9

Discrete-Time Neural Observers. DOI: 10.1016/B978-0-12-810543-6.00002-2

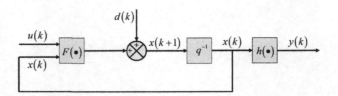

FIGURE 2.1 Schematic representation of a nonlinear system.

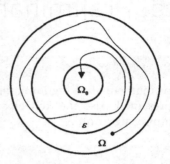

FIGURE 2.2 SGUUB, schematic representation.

Such a substitution eliminates u,

$$\chi(k+1) = F(\chi(k), \xi(x(k))),\qquad(2.5)$$

and yields the unforced system (2.3).

Definition 2.2 ([7]). The solution of (2.3) is said to be semiglobally uniformly ultimately bounded (SGUUB), if for any Ω, a compact subset of $\Re^n$ and all $x(k_0) \in \Omega$, there exists an $\varepsilon > 0$ and a number $N(\varepsilon, x(k_0))$ such that $\|x(k)\| < \varepsilon$ for all $k \geq k_0 + N$.

In other words, the solution of (2.1) is said to be SGUUB if, for any a priori given (arbitrarily large) bounded set Ω and any a priori given (arbitrarily small) set Ω_0, which contains $(0, 0)$ as an interior point, there exists a control (2.4) such that every trajectory of the closed loop system starting from Ω enters the set $\Omega_0 = \{x(k) \mid \|x(k)\| < \varepsilon\}$ in finite time and remains there thereafter, as is displayed in Fig. 2.2.

Theorem 2.1 ([7]). *Let $V(x(k))$ be a Lyapunov function for a discrete-time system (2.1), which satisfies the following properties:*

$$\gamma_1(\|x(k)\|) \leq V(x(k)) \leq \gamma_2(\|x(k)\|),$$
$$V(x(k+1)) - V(x(k)) = \Delta V(x(k))$$
$$\leq -\gamma_3(\|x(k)\|) + \gamma_3(\zeta)$$

where ζ is a positive constant, $\gamma_1(\bullet)$ and $\gamma_2(\bullet)$ are strictly increasing functions, and $\gamma_3(\bullet)$ is a continuous, nondecreasing function. Thus if

$$\Delta V(x) < 0 \quad for \quad \|x(k)\| > \zeta$$

then $x(k)$ is uniformly ultimately bounded, i.e., there is a time instant k_T such that $\|x(k)\| < \zeta, \forall\, k < k_T$.

Definition 2.3 ([10]). A subset $S \in \Re^n$ is bounded if there exists $r > 0$ such that $\|x\| \leq r$ for all $x \in S$.

2.2 INTRODUCTION TO ARTIFICIAL NEURAL NETWORKS

Artificial neural networks have become a useful tool for control engineering thanks to their applicability in modeling, state estimation, and control of complex dynamic systems. Using neural networks, control algorithms can be developed to be robust to uncertainties and modeling errors.

A neural networks consist of a number of interconnected processing elements, or neurons. The way in which the neurons are interconnected determines its structure. The most used structures are:

Feedforward networks In such networks, the neurons are grouped into layers. Signals flow from the input to the output via unidirectional connections. The network exhibits high degree of connectivity, contains one or more hidden layers of neurons, and the activation function of each neuron is smooth, generally a sigmoid function.

Recurrent networks In such networks, the outputs of the neuron are fed back to the same neuron or neurons in the preceding layers. Signals flow in forward and backward directions.

2.2.1 The Neuron

The neuron (also named a node or unit) is a processing element which takes a number of inputs, weights them, sums them up, and uses the result as the argument for a singular-valued function, the activation function, as shown in Fig. 2.3.

From Fig. 2.3, it is possible to identify four basic elements of the neural model:

1. A set of synapses or connecting links, each of which is characterized by a weight or its own strength. Specifically, a signal x_j at the input synapse j connected to neuron k is multiplied by the synaptic weight w_{kj}. Unlike the synapse in the brain, the synaptic weight of an artificial neuron may lie in a range that includes negative as well as positive values.
2. An externally applied bias, denoted by b_k, which increases or decreases the net input of the activation function, depending on its value.

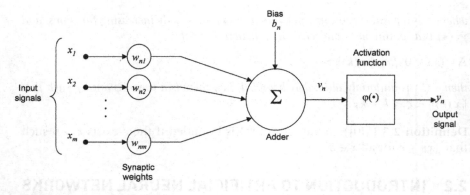

FIGURE 2.3 Artificial neuron model.

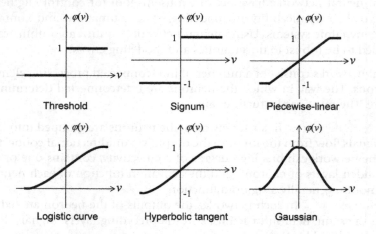

FIGURE 2.4 Common activation functions.

3. An adder for summing the input signals, weighted by the respective synapses of the neuron; the operation performed in this element constitutes a linear combiner.
4. An activation function for limiting the amplitude of the output of a neuron. The activation functions are selected specific to the applications though some common choices as illustrated in Fig. 2.4. The intent of the activation function is to model the nonlinear behavior of the cell where there is no output below a certain value of the argument [17].

2.2.2 Feedforward Neural Networks

Artificial neural network units (neurons) can be combined in different ways and this fact is intimately linked with the learning algorithm used to train them [14]. Commonly, neurons in a network are organized in layers. In the simplest

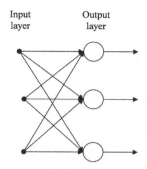

FIGURE 2.5 Scheme for a single layer neural network.

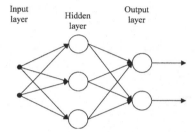

FIGURE 2.6 Scheme for a multilayer neural network.

form of a neural network, it is possible to find an input layer of source nodes which projects onto an output layer of neurons (computation nodes), but not vice versa. In other words, this kind of neural network is strictly feedforward or acyclic. It is illustrated in Fig. 2.5 for the case of three nodes in both the input and output layers. Such a network is called a single-layer network; such designation refers to the output layer of neurons. The input layer is not taken into account due the fact that there are no neurons in it; therefore, no computation is performed there [9].

Another class of feedforward neural network distinguishes itself by the presence of one or more hidden layers, whose computation nodes are correspondingly called hidden neurons or hidden units. The function of hidden neurons is to intervene between the external input and the network output in a useful manner. By adding one or more hidden layers, the network is able to extract important characteristics from input data, which is particularly valuable when the size of the input layer is large [9]. The source nodes in the input layer of the network supply respective elements of the activation pattern (input vector), which constitute the input signals applied to the neurons in the second layer. The output signals of the second layer are used as inputs of the third layer, and so on, for the rest of the network. Fig. 2.6 illustrates the layout of a multilayer feedforward neural network for the case of a single hidden layer. This neural

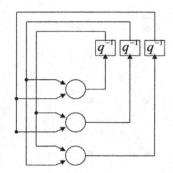

FIGURE 2.7 Scheme for a recurrent neural network without self-feedback loops.

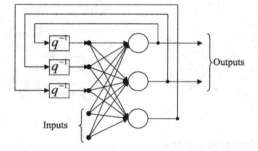

FIGURE 2.8 Scheme for a recurrent neural network with self-feedback loops.

network is said to be fully connected in the sense that every node in each layer of the network is connected to every other node in the adjacent forward layer. If, however, some of the synaptic weight are missing from the network, it is known as partially connected [9]. The use of multilayer neural networks is well known for pattern recognition and for modeling of static systems. The NN is trained to learn an input–output map. Theoretical results [3,9] establish that, even with just one hidden layer, an NN can uniformly approximate any continuous function over a compact domain, provided that the NN has a sufficient number of synaptic connections [9].

2.2.3 Recurrent Neural Networks

A recurrent neural network distinguishes itself from a feedforward one in that it has at least one feedback loop. For example, a recurrent network may consist of a single layer of neurons with each neuron feeding its output signal back to the inputs of all other neurons, as illustrated in Fig. 2.7. In the structure depicted in this figure, there are no self-feedback loops in the network; self-feedback refers to a situation where the output of a neuron is fed back into its own input, as is shown in Fig. 2.8.

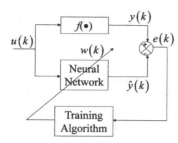

FIGURE 2.9 Schematic representation for an online neural approximation.

The presence of feedback loops in a neural network has a profound impact on the learning capability of the network and on its performance. Moreover, feedback loops in a neural network result in a nonlinear dynamical behavior due to the use of nonlinear activation functions. This kind of neural network allows better understanding of biological structures, and can offer also great computational advantages. It is well known that feedforward (or static) neural networks are capable of approximating any continuous function [3]. However, the recurrent neural networks possess a rich repertoire of architectures, which qualifies them for various applications not possible with feedforward ones; some of these applications are nonlinear prediction, modeling, control, state space representation, among others.

The dynamic behavior of recurrent neural networks is due to the inclusion of recurrent connections, which facilitate the processing of temporal information or dynamic patterns, i.e., time-dependent patterns in the sense that the standard value at a given time depends on past values.

2.3 DISCRETE-TIME HIGH ORDER NEURAL NETWORKS

Artificial Recurrent Neural Networks are mostly based on the Hopfield model [16]. These networks are considered good candidates for nonlinear systems applications which deal with uncertainties and are attractive due to their easy implementation, relatively simple structure, robustness, and the capacity to adjust their parameters online. Fig. 2.9 shows a schematic representation of an online neural network to approximate an unknown nonlinear function f with input u and output y. The neural network adapts its weights w online in order to minimize a functional of the error e between the function output y and the neural network output $\widehat{y}$.

For control systems, extensions of the first order Hopfield model called Recurrent High Order Neural Networks (RHONN), which present more interconnections among neurons, are proposed in [13,16]. Additionally, the RHONN model is very flexible and allows incorporating to the neural model a priori information about the system structure, such as input signals and control systems, among others.

Define the following discrete-time recurrent high order neural network (RHONN):

$$\widehat{x}(k+1) = w_i^\top z_i(\widehat{x}(k), u(k)), \quad i = 1, \ldots, n \tag{2.6}$$

where $\widehat{x}_i$ $(i = 1, 2, \ldots, n)$ is the state of the ith neuron, L_i is the respective number of high-order connections, $\{I_1, I_2, \ldots, I_{L_i}\}$ is a collection of unordered subsets of $\{1, 2, \ldots, n+m\}$, n is the state dimension, m is the number of external inputs, w_i $(i = 1, 2, \ldots, n)$ is the respective online adapted weight vector, and $z_i(\widehat{x}(k), u(k))$ is given by

$$z_i(\widehat{x}(k), u(k)) = \begin{bmatrix} z_{i_1} \\ z_{i_2} \\ \vdots \\ z_{i_{L_i}} \end{bmatrix} = \begin{bmatrix} \Pi_{j \in I_1} \xi_{i_j}^{d_{ij}(1)} \\ \Pi_{j \in I_2} \xi_{i_j}^{d_{ij}(2)} \\ \vdots \\ \Pi_{j \in I_{L_i}} \xi_{i_j}^{d_{ij}(L_i)} \end{bmatrix} \tag{2.7}$$

with $d_{j_i}(k)$ being nonnegative integers, and ξ_i defined as follows:

$$\xi_i = \begin{bmatrix} \xi_{i_1} \\ \vdots \\ \xi_{i_1} \\ \xi_{i_{n+1}} \\ \vdots \\ \xi_{i_{n+m}} \end{bmatrix} = \begin{bmatrix} S(\widehat{x}_1) \\ \vdots \\ S(\widehat{x}_n) \\ u_1 \\ \vdots \\ u_m \end{bmatrix}. \tag{2.8}$$

In (2.8), $u = [u_1, u_2, \ldots, u_m]^\top$ is the input vector to the neural network, and $S(\bullet)$ is defined by

$$S(\varsigma) = \frac{1}{1 + \exp(-\beta\varsigma)}, \quad \beta > 0 \tag{2.9}$$

where ς is any real value variable.

From (2.6) three possible models can be derived:

- Parallel model, schematic representation of which is included in Fig. 2.10,

$$\widehat{x}_i(k+1) = w_i^\top z_i(\widehat{x}(k), u(k)), \quad i = 1, \ldots, n; \tag{2.10}$$

- Series–parallel model, schematic representation of which is included in Fig. 2.11,

$$\widehat{x}_i(k+1) = w_i^\top z_i(x(k), u(k)), \quad i = 1, \ldots, n; \tag{2.11}$$

- Feedforward model (HONN), schematic representation of which is included in Fig. 2.12,

$$\widehat{x}_i(k) = w_i^\top z_i(u(k)), \quad i = 1, \ldots, n, \tag{2.12}$$

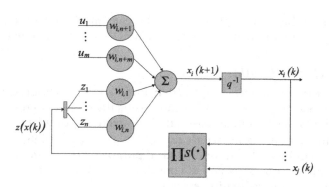

FIGURE 2.10 Schematic representation for an RHONN in a parallel model.

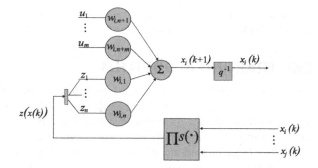

FIGURE 2.11 Schematic representation for an RHONN in a series–parallel model.

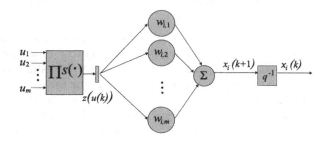

FIGURE 2.12 Schematic representation for an HONN in a feedforward model.

where $\hat{x}$ is the NN state vector, x is the plant state vector, and u is the input vector to the NN.

It is important to note that a disadvantage of this type of NN is that there does not exist, to the best of our knowledge, a methodology to determine its structure; thus, it has to be selected experimentally.

Consider the problem of approximating the general discrete-time nonlinear system (2.1), by the following discrete-time RHONN series–parallel representation [16]:

$$x_i(k+1) = w_i^{*\top} z_i(\widehat{x}(k), u(k)) + \epsilon_{z_i}, \quad i = 1, \ldots, n, \tag{2.13}$$

where x_i is the ith plant state, $\widehat{x}_i$ is the ith neural state, ϵ_{z_i} is a bounded approximation error, which can be reduced by increasing the number of the adjustable weights [16]. Assume that there exists an ideal weight vector w_i^* such that $\|\epsilon_{z_i}\|$ can be minimized on a compact set $\Omega_{z_i} \subset \Re^{L_i}$. The ideal weight vector w_i^* is an artificial quantity required for analytical purposes [16]. In general, it is assumed that this vector exists and is constant but unknown. Let us define its estimate as w_i and the estimation error as

$$\widetilde{w}_i(k) = w_i^* - w_i(k). \tag{2.14}$$

The estimate w_i is used for stability analysis, which will be discussed later. Since w_i^* is constant, $\widetilde{w}_i(k+1) - \widetilde{w}_i(k) = w_i(k+1) - w_i(k)$, $\forall k \in 0 \cup \mathbb{Z}^+$.

2.4 THE EKF TRAINING ALGORITHM

The best well-known training approach for recurrent neural networks (RNN) is the back propagation through time learning [20]. However, it is a first order gradient descent method and hence its learning speed could be very slow [12]; besides, this training approach can experience a local minimum [9]. Recently, Extended Kalman Filter (EKF) based algorithms have been introduced to train neural networks [1,6]. With the EKF based algorithm, the learning convergence is improved [12]. The EKF training of neural networks, both feedforward and recurrent, has proven to be reliable and practical for many applications over the past ten years [6].

It is known that Kalman filtering (KF) estimates the state of a linear system with additive state and output white noises [8,18]. For KF-based neural network training, the network weights become the states to be estimated. In this case, the error between the neural network output and the measured plant output can be considered as additive white noise. Due to the fact that the neural network mapping is nonlinear, an EKF-type is required (see [15] and references therein). Fig. 2.13 depicts a diagram of the update process for the extended Kalman Filter.

The training goal is to find the optimal weight values which minimize the prediction error $(y(k) - \widehat{y}(k))$. The EKF-based training algorithm is described by [8]:

$$\begin{aligned}
K_i(k) &= P_i(k) H_i(k) \left[R_i(k) + H_i^\top(k) P_i(k) H_i(k) \right]^{-1}, \\
w_i(k+1) &= w_i(k) + \eta_i K_i(k) \left[y(k) - \widehat{y}(k) \right], \\
P_i(k+1) &= P_i(k) - K_i(k) H_i^\top(k) P_i(k) + Q_i(k)
\end{aligned} \tag{2.15}$$

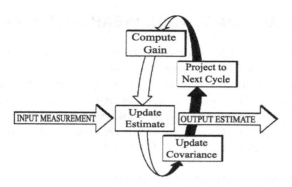

FIGURE 2.13 Update process for extended Kalman filter.

where $P_i \in \Re^{L_i \times L_i}$ is the prediction error associated covariance matrix, $w_i \in \Re^{L_i}$ is the weight (state) vector, L_i is the total number of neural network weights, $y \in \Re^m$ is the measured output vector, $\widehat{y} \in \Re^m$ is the network output, η_i is a design parameter, $K_i \in \Re^{L_i \times m}$ is the Kalman gain matrix, $Q_i \in \Re^{L_i \times L_i}$ is the state noise associated covariance matrix, $R_i \in \Re^{m \times m}$ is the measurement noise associated covariance matrix, $H_i \in \Re^{L_i \times m}$ is a matrix, for which each entry (H_{ij}) is the derivative of one of the neural network output, $(\widehat{y})$, with respect to one neural network weight, (w_{ij}), as follows:

$$H_{ij}(k) = \left[\frac{\partial \widehat{y}(k)}{\partial w_{ij}(k)} \right]_{w_i(k)=\widehat{w}_i(k+1)} \quad , \quad i = 1, \ldots, n \text{ and } j = 1, \ldots, L_i. \qquad (2.16)$$

Usually, P_i, Q_i, and R_i are initialized as diagonal matrices with entries $P_i(0)$, $Q_i(0)$, and $R_i(0)$, respectively. It is important to note that $H_i(k)$, $K_i(k)$, and $P_i(k)$ for the EKF are bounded [18]. Therefore, there exist constants $\overline{H}_i > 0$, $\overline{K}_i > 0$, and $\overline{P}_i > 0$ such that:

$$\|H_i(k)\| \leq \overline{H}_i,$$
$$\|K_i(k)\| \leq \overline{K}_i, \qquad (2.17)$$
$$\|P_i(k)\| \leq \overline{P}_i.$$

The measurement and process noises are typically characterized as zero-mean, white noises with covariances given by $\delta_{k,j} R_i(k)$ and $\delta_{k,j} Q_i(k)$, respectively, with $\delta_{k,j}$ being the Kronecker delta function (0 for $k \neq l$ and 1 for $k = l$) [9]. To simplify the notation, in this book the covariances will be represented by their respective associated matrices, $R_i(k)$ and $Q_i(k)$, for the noises and $P_i(k)$ for the prediction error.

2.5 INTRODUCTION TO NONLINEAR OBSERVERS

During the past four decades, state estimation of dynamical systems has been an active topic of research in different areas, such as automatic control applications, fault detection, monitoring, and modeling, among others [4]. This fact is due to that nonlinear control techniques usually assume complete accessibility for the system state, which is not always possible (cost, technological constraints, etc.) [2]. For this reason, nonlinear state estimation is a very important topic for nonlinear control [5,11,15,19].

2.5.1 Observer Problem Statement

Given the system (2.1)–(2.2), for the purpose of acting on it or monitoring it we will, in general, need to know $x(k)$, while in practice it is only possible to access u and y. The observation problem can then be formulated as follows [2]:

Given a system described by a representation (2.1)–(2.2), find an estimate $\widehat{x}(k)$ for $x(k)$ from the knowledge of $u(\tau)$, $y(\tau)$ for $0 \leq \varsigma \leq k$.

Clearly, this problem makes sense when it is not possible to invert $h(\bullet)$ w.r.t. $x(\bullet)$ at any time. First, it is possible to search for a solution in terms of optimization, by looking for the best estimate $\widehat{x}(0)$ of $x(0)$ which can explain the evolution $y(k)$ over $[0, k]$, and then from this get an estimate $x(k)$ by solving (2.1)–(2.2) from $\widehat{x}(0)$ and under the action of $u(\tau)$. In order to cope with disturbances, it is necessary to optimize the estimate of some initial state over a moving horizon with a criterion like the mean squared error [2]. This approach is a general formulation, relying on available optimization tools; so it takes advantage of the systematic formulation, but suffers from usual drawbacks of nonlinear optimization (computational burden, local minima, etc.) [2].

Alternatively, it is possible to use the idea of an explicit feedback to estimate $\widehat{x}(k)$, as is done for control purposes: more precisely, by noting that if the initial value $\widehat{x}(0)$ is known, then it is possible to get an estimate for $\widehat{x}(k)$ by solving (2.1)–(2.2) from $\widehat{x}(0)$. The feedback-based idea is that if $\widehat{x}(0)$ is unknown, it is possible to correct the estimation error online, by solving $\widehat{x}(k)$ in (2.1)–(2.2) from some erroneous $\widehat{x}(0)$, according to the measurable error $h(\widehat{x}(k)) - y(k)$, with $y(k) = h(x(k))$, namely to look for an estimate $\widehat{x}(k)$ of $x(k)$ as the solution of:

$$\widehat{x}(k+1) = F(\widehat{x}(k), u(k)) + L(k, h(\widehat{x}(k)) - y(k)) \quad \text{with } L(k, 0) = 0.$$

Such an auxiliary system is defined as an observer (see Fig. 2.14), and the above equation is its most common form for (2.1)–(2.2) [2].

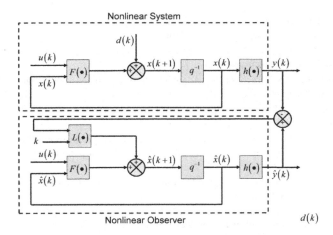

FIGURE 2.14 Schematic representation of a general nonlinear observer.

REFERENCES

[1] A.Y. Alanis, E.N. Sanchez, A.G. Loukianov, Discrete time adaptive backstepping nonlinear control via high order neural networks, IEEE Transactions on Neural Networks 18 (4) (July 2007) 1185–1195.

[2] G. Besançon, Nonlinear Observers and Applications, LNCIS, vol. 363, Springer-Verlag, Berlin, Germany, 2007.

[3] N.E. Cotter, The Stone–Weierstrass theorem and its application to neural networks, IEEE Transactions on Neural Networks 1 (1990).

[4] D.F. Coutinho, L.P.F.A. Pereira, A robust Luenberger-like observer for induction machines, in: Proceedings IEEE IECON 2005, Nov. 2005.

[5] J.A. Farrell, M.M. Polycarpou, Adaptive Approximation Based Control: Unifying Neural, Fuzzy and Traditional Adaptive Approximation Approaches, John Wiley and Sons, NY, USA, 2006.

[6] L.A. Feldkamp, D.V. Prokhorov, T.M. Feldkamp, Simple and conditioned adaptive behavior from Kalman filter trained recurrent networks, Neural Networks 16 (2003) 683–689.

[7] S.S. Ge, J. Zhang, T.H. Lee, Adaptive neural network control for a class of MIMO nonlinear systems with disturbances in discrete-time, IEEE Transactions on Systems, Man and Cybernetics, Part B 34 (4) (Aug. 2004).

[8] R. Grover, P.Y.C. Hwang, Introduction to Random Signals and Applied Kalman Filtering, 2nd ed., John Wiley and Sons, New York, USA, 1992.

[9] S. Haykin, Kalman Filtering and Neural Networks, John Wiley and Sons, NY, USA, 2001.

[10] H. Khalil, Nonlinear Systems, 2nd ed., Prentice Hall, Upper Saddle River, NJ, USA, 1996.

[11] Y.H. Kim, F.L. Lewis, High-Level Feedback Control with Neural Networks, World Scientific, Singapore, 1998.

[12] C. Leunga, L. Chan, Dual extended Kalman filtering in recurrent neural networks, Neural Networks 16 (2003) 223–239.

[13] K.S. Narendra, K. Parthasarathy, Identification and control of dynamical systems using neural networks, IEEE Transactions on Neural Networks 1 (Mar. 1990) 4–27.

[14] M. Nørgaard, O. Ravn, N.K. Poulsen, L.K. Hansen, Neural Networks for Modelling and Control of Dynamic Systems, Springer-Verlag, London, 2000.

[15] A.S. Poznyak, E.N. Sanchez, W. Yu, Differential Neural Networks for Robust Nonlinear Control, World Scientific, Singapore, 2001.

[16] G.A. Rovithakis, M.A. Chistodoulou, Adaptive Control with Recurrent High-Order Neural Networks, Springer-Verlag, New York, USA, 2000.

[17] J. Sarangapani, Neural Network Control of Nonlinear Discrete-Time Systems, CRC Press, Taylor & Francis Group, Boca Raton, FL, USA, 2006.

[18] Y. Song, J.W. Grizzle, The extended Kalman filter as local asymptotic observer for discrete-time nonlinear systems, Journal of Mathematical Systems, Estimation, and Control 5 (1) (1995) 59–78.

[19] V. Utkin, J. Guldner, J. Shi, Sliding Mode Control in Electromechanical Systems, Taylor and Francis, Philadelphia, USA, 1999.

[20] R.J. Williams, D. Zipser, A learning algorithm for continually running fully recurrent neural networks, Neural Computation 1 (1989) 270–280.

CHAPTER 3

Full Order Neural Observers

ABSTRACT

In this chapter, the Neural Observer scheme is introduced for unknown discrete-time MIMO nonlinear systems with linear output; then a similar scheme is proposed for unknown discrete-time MIMO nonlinear systems with nonlinear outputs. To illustrate the applicability of the proposed neural observers, four meaningful applications are included at the end of this chapter: human immunodeficiency virus (HIV), rotatory induction motors, linear induction motors, and anaerobic digestion.

KEYWORDS

Full order observers

Neural observers

Unknown discrete-time nonlinear systems

Human immunodeficiency virus (HIV)

Rotatory induction motors

Linear induction motors

Anaerobic digestion

CONTENTS

3.1 LINEAR OUTPUT CASE

In this section, we consider estimating the state of a discrete-time nonlinear system (Fig. 3.1), which is assumed to be observable, given by

$$x(k+1) = F(x(k), u(k)) + d(k),$$
$$y(k) = Cx(k) \qquad (3.1)$$

where $x \in \Re^n$ is the state vector of the system, $u(k) \in \Re^m$ is the input vector, $y(k) \in \Re^p$ is the output vector, $C \in \Re^{p \times n}$ is a known output matrix, $d(k) \in \Re^n$ is a disturbance vector, and $F(\bullet)$ is a smooth vector field, with $f_i(\bullet)$ as its entries; hence (3.1) can be rewritten as:

$$x(k) = \begin{bmatrix} x_1(k) & \dots & x_i(k) & \dots & x_n(k) \end{bmatrix}^\top,$$

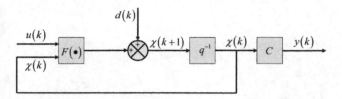

FIGURE 3.1 Schematic representation for an unknown discrete-time nonlinear system with linear output.

$$d(k) = \left[\ d_1(k)\ \ \dots\ \ d_i(k)\ \ \dots\ \ d_n(k)\ \right]^{\top},$$
$$x_i(k+1) = f_i(x(k), u(k)) + d_i(k), \quad i = 1, \dots, n,$$
$$y(k) = Cx(k). \tag{3.2}$$

For system (3.2), we propose a recurrent neural Luenberger type observer (RHONO) with the following structure:

$$\widehat{x}(k) = \left[\ \widehat{x}_1(k)\ \ \dots\ \ \widehat{x}_i(k)\ \ \dots\ \ \widehat{x}_n(k)\ \right]^{\top},$$
$$\widehat{x}_i(k+1) = w_i^{\top} z_i(\widehat{x}(k), u(k)) + g_i e(k),$$
$$\widehat{y}(k) = C\widehat{x}(k), \quad i = 1, \dots, n, \tag{3.3}$$

with $g_i \in \Re^p$, w_i and $z_i(x(k), u(k))$ as defined in (2.6) and (2.7), respectively.

As discussed in [4], the general discrete-time nonlinear system (3.1), which is assumed to be observable, can be approximated by the following discrete-time RHONN parallel representation:

$$x(k+1) = W^{*\top} z(x(k), u(k)) + \epsilon_z, \tag{3.4}$$

or in the component-wise form

$$x_i(k+1) = w_i^{*\top} z_i(x(k), u(k)) + \epsilon_{z_i}, \quad i = 1, \dots, n, \tag{3.5}$$

where x_i is the ith plant state and ϵ_{z_i} is a bounded approximation error, which can be reduced by increasing the number of the adjustable weights [4]. Assume that there exists an ideal weight vector $w_i^* \in \Re^{L_i}$ such that $\|\epsilon_{z_i}\|$ can be minimized on a compact set $\Omega_{z_i} \subset \Re^{L_i}$. w_i^* is an artificial quantity only required for analytical purposes [4]. In general, it is assumed that this vector exists and is constant but unknown. Let us define its estimate as w_i. Then the weights estimate $\widetilde{w}_i(k)$ and state observer $\widetilde{x}_i(k)$ errors are respectively defined as

$$\widetilde{w}_i(k) = w_i^* - w_i(k) \tag{3.6}$$

and

$$\widetilde{x}_i(k) = x_i(k) - \widehat{x}_i(k). \tag{3.7}$$

Since w_i^* is constant, then

$$\widetilde{w}_i(k+1) - \widetilde{w}_i(k) = w_i(k+1) - w_i(k), \quad \forall k \in 0 \cup \mathbb{Z}^+.$$

The weight vectors are updated online with a decoupled EKF [2], described by

$$w_i(k+1) = w_i(k) + \eta_i K_i(k) e(k), \tag{3.8}$$
$$K_i(k) = P_i(k) H_i(k) M_i(k),$$
$$P_i(k+1) = P_i(k) - K_i(k) H_i^\top(k) P_i(k) + Q_i(k), \quad i = 1, \ldots, n,$$

with

$$M_i(k) = \left[R_i(k) + H_i^\top(k) P_i(k) H_i(k) \right]^{-1}. \tag{3.9}$$

The output error is defined by

$$e(k) = y(k) - \widehat{y}(k), \tag{3.10}$$

and the state estimation error is

$$\widetilde{x}(k) = x(k) - \widehat{x}(k). \tag{3.11}$$

Then the dynamics of (3.7) can be expressed as

$$\widetilde{x}(k+1) = x(k+1) - \widehat{x}(k+1). \tag{3.12}$$

Substituting (3.3) and (3.5) into (3.12) yields

$$\widetilde{x}_i(k+1) = \widetilde{w}_i(k) z_i(\widehat{x}(k), u(k)) + \epsilon'_{z_i} - g_i C \widetilde{x}(k) \tag{3.13}$$

with $\epsilon'_{z_i} = w_i^{*T} z_i(\widetilde{x}(k), u(k)) + \epsilon_{z_i}$ and $z_i(\widetilde{x}(k), u(k)) = z_i(x(k), u(k)) - z_i(\widehat{x}(k), u(k))$. On the other hand, the dynamics of (3.6) can be expressed as

$$\widetilde{w}_i(k+1) = w_i(k+1) - w_i^*. \tag{3.14}$$

Using (3.8) in (3.14), it is possible to obtain

$$\widetilde{w}_i(k+1) = \widetilde{w}_i(k) - \eta_i K_i(k) e(k). \tag{3.15}$$

The proposed neural observer scheme is presented in Fig. 3.2.

Considering (3.8)–(3.15), we establish the first main result of this chapter as the following theorem.

Theorem 3.1. *For system (3.2), the RHONO (3.3), trained with the EKF-based algorithm (3.8), ensures that the ith ($i = 1, 2, \ldots, n$) estimation error (3.11) and the output error (3.10) are semi-globally uniformly ultimately bounded (SGUUB); moreover, the RHONO weights remain bounded.*

Proof. Consider the candidate Lyapunov function

$$V_i(k) = \widetilde{w}_i^T(k) P_i(k) \widetilde{w}_i(k) + \widetilde{x}_i^T(k) \widetilde{x}_i(k) \tag{3.16}$$

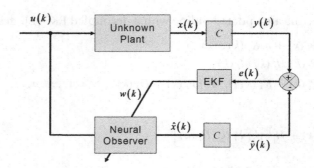

FIGURE 3.2 Neural observer scheme for linear output.

whose first increment is defined as

$$
\begin{aligned}
\Delta V_i\,(k) &= V_i\,(k+1) - V_i\,(k) \\
&= \widetilde{w}_i^T\,(k+1)\,P_i\,(k+1)\,\widetilde{w}_i\,(k+1) + \widetilde{x}_i^T\,(k+1)\,\widetilde{x}_i\,(k+1) \\
&\quad - \widetilde{w}_i^T\,(k)\,P_i\,(k)\,\widetilde{w}_i\,(k) - \widetilde{x}_i^T\,(k)\,\widetilde{x}_i\,(k)\,.
\end{aligned}
\tag{3.17}
$$

Substituting (3.2), (3.13) and (3.15) into (3.17) yields

$$
\begin{aligned}
\Delta V_i\,(k) &= \big[\widetilde{w}_i\,(k) - \eta_i\,K_i\,(k)\,C\widetilde{x}\,(k)\big]^T \big[A_i\,(k)\big]\big[\widetilde{w}_i\,(k) - \eta_i\,K_i\,(k)\,C\widetilde{x}\,(k)\big] \\
&\quad + \big[f_i\,(k) - g_i\,C\widetilde{x}\,(k)\big]^T \big[f_i\,(k) - g_i\,C\widetilde{x}\,(k)\big] \\
&\quad - \widetilde{w}_i^T\,(k)\,P_i\,(k)\,\widetilde{w}_i\,(k) - \widetilde{x}_i^T\,(k)\,\widetilde{x}_i\,(k) \\
&= -\widetilde{w}_i^T\,(k)\,B_i\,(k)\,\widetilde{w}_i\,(k) - \eta_i\,\widetilde{x}^T\,(k)\,C^T\,K_i^T\,(k)\,A_i\,(k)\,\widetilde{w}_i\,(k) \\
&\quad - \eta_i\,\widetilde{w}_i^T\,(k)\,A_i\,(k)\,C\widetilde{x}\,(k) + \eta_i^2\,\widetilde{x}^T\,(k)\,C^T\,K_i^T\,(k)\,A_i\,(k)\,K_i\,(k)\,C\widetilde{x}\,(k) \\
&\quad + f_i^T\,(k)\,f_i\,(k) - f_i^T\,(k)\,g_i\,C\widetilde{x}\,(k) - \widetilde{x}^T\,(k)\,C^T\,g_i^T\,f_i\,(k) \\
&\quad + \widetilde{x}^T\,(k)\,C^T\,g_i^T\,g_i\,C\widetilde{x}\,(k) - \widetilde{x}_i^T\,(k)\,\widetilde{x}_i\,(k)
\end{aligned}
\tag{3.18}
$$

with

$$
\begin{aligned}
A_i\,(k) &= P_i\,(k) - B_i\,(k)\,, \\
B_i\,(k) &= K_i\,(k)\,H_i^T\,(k)\,P_i\,(k) + Q_i\,(k)\,, \\
f_i\,(k) &= \widetilde{w}_i^T\,(k)\,z_i\,(\widehat{x}(k),\,u(k)) + \epsilon_{z_i}'\,.
\end{aligned}
$$

Using the following inequalities:

$$
X^T X + Y^T Y \geq -X^T Y - Y^T X,
$$
$$
-\lambda_{\min}\,(P)\,X^2 \geq -X^T P X \geq -\lambda_{\max}\,(P)\,X^2,
$$

which are valid $\forall X, Y \in \Re^n$, $\forall P \in \Re^{n \times n}$, $P = P^T > 0$, expression (3.18) can be rewritten as

$$
\Delta V_i\,(k) \leq -\|\widetilde{w}_i\,(k)\|^2\,\lambda_{\min}\,(B_i\,(k)) + 2\,\|f_i\,(k)\|^2
$$

$$+ \eta_i^2 \|\widetilde{x}(k)\|^2 \|C\|^2 \|K_i(k)\|^2 \lambda_{\max} A_i(k)$$
$$+ 2 \|\widetilde{x}(k)\|^2 \|C\|^2 \|g_i\|^2 - \|\widetilde{x}(k)\|^2$$
$$+ \|K_i(k)\|^2 \|A_i(k)\|^2 \|\widetilde{w}_i(k)\|^2 + \eta_i^2 \|\widetilde{x}(k)\|^2 \|C\|^2. \tag{3.19}$$

Replacing $f_i(k)$ in (3.19) gives

$$\Delta V_i(k) \leq - \|\widetilde{w}_i(k)\|^2 \lambda_{\min}(B_i(k)) + 2 \|\widetilde{w}_i(k)\|^2 \|z_i(\widehat{x}(k), u(k))\|^2$$
$$+ \eta_i^2 \|\widetilde{x}(k)\|^2 \|C\|^2 \|K_i(k)\|^2 \lambda_{\max} A_i(k)$$
$$+ 2 \|\widetilde{x}(k)\|^2 \|C\|^2 \|g_i\|^2 - \|\widetilde{x}(k)\|^2 + \eta_i^2 \|\widetilde{x}(k)\|^2 \|C\|^2$$
$$+ \|K_i(k)\|^2 \|A_i(k)\|^2 \|\widetilde{w}_i(k)\|^2 + 2 |\epsilon'_{z_i}|^2. \tag{3.20}$$

Defining

$$E_i(k) = \lambda_{\min}(B_i(k)) - \|K_i(k)\|^2 \|A_i(k)\|^2 - 2 \|z_i(\widehat{x}(k), u(k))\|^2, \tag{3.21}$$
$$F_i(k) = 1 - \eta_i^2 \|C\|^2 \|K_i(k)\|^2 \lambda_{\max} A_i(k) - 2 \|C\|^2 \|g_i\|^2 - \eta_i^2 \|C\|^2, \tag{3.22}$$

one can express (3.20) as

$$\Delta V_i(k) \leq - \|\widetilde{w}_i(k)\|^2 E_i(k) - \|\widetilde{x}(k)\|^2 F_i(k) + 2 |\epsilon'_{z_i}|^2.$$

Hence, $\Delta V_i(k) < 0$, whenever

$$\|\widetilde{x}(k)\|^2 > \sqrt{\frac{2 |\epsilon'_{z_i}|^2}{F_i(k)}},$$

or

$$\|\widetilde{w}_i(k)\|^2 > \sqrt{\frac{2 |\epsilon'_{z_i}|^2}{E_i(k)}}.$$

Therefore, the solution of (3.13) and (3.15) is stable; hence the estimation error and the RHONN weights are SGUUB. Now, to proceed with the proof, consider the Lyapunov function candidate

$$V_i(k) = \sum_{i=1}^{n} (\widetilde{w}_i(k) P_i(k) \widetilde{w}_i(k) + \widetilde{x}_i(k) \widetilde{x}_i(k)) \tag{3.23}$$

whose first increment is defined as

$$\Delta V_i(k) = \sum_{i=1}^{n} (\widetilde{w}_i(k+1) P_i(k+1) \widetilde{w}_i(k+1)$$
$$+ \widetilde{x}_i(k+1) \widetilde{x}_i(k+1)$$
$$- \widetilde{w}_i(k) P_i(k) \widetilde{w}_i(k)$$
$$- \widetilde{x}_i(k) P_i(k) \widetilde{x}_i(k)). \tag{3.24}$$

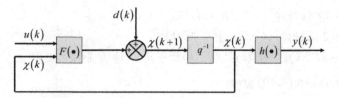

FIGURE 3.3 Schematic representation for an unknown discrete-time nonlinear system with non-linear output.

Therefore, as above, (3.24) can be expressed as

$$\Delta V_i(k) \le \sum_{i=1}^{n} \left(-\|\widetilde{w}_i(k)\|^2 E_i(k) - \|\widetilde{x}(k)\|^2 F_i(k) + 2\left|\epsilon'_{z_i}\right|^2 \right)$$

with $E_i(k)$ and $F_i(k)$ as in (3.21) and (3.22), respectively. As a result, $\Delta V_i(k) < 0$ when

$$\|\widetilde{x}(k)\| > \kappa_1(k)$$

or

$$\|\widetilde{w}_i(k)\| > \kappa_2(k),$$

and if $\|\widetilde{x}(k)\| > \kappa_1(k)$ and $\|\widetilde{w}_i(k)\| > \kappa_2(k)$, $\forall i = 1, \ldots, n$ holds, then $\Delta V_i(k) < 0$. Finally, considering (3.10) and (3.11), it is easy to see that the output error has an algebraic relation with $\widetilde{x}(k)$, and for that reason, if $\widetilde{x}(k)$ is bounded, $e(k)$ is bounded, too:

$$e(k) = y(k) - \widehat{y}(k) = Cx(k) - C\widehat{x}(k) = C\widetilde{x}(k),$$
$$\|e(k)\| = \|C\| \|\widetilde{x}(k)\|. \qquad \square$$

3.2 NONLINEAR OUTPUT CASE

In this section, we consider estimating the state of a discrete-time nonlinear system (Fig. 3.3), which is assumed to be observable, given by

$$x(k+1) = F(x(k), u(k)) + d(k),$$
$$y(k) = h(x(k)) \qquad (3.25)$$

where $x \in \Re^n$ is the state vector of the system, $u(k) \in \Re^m$ is the input vector, $y(k) \in \Re^p$ is the output vector, $h(\bullet)$ is a known nonlinear output function, which is Lipschitz in $x(k)$, $d(k) \in \Re^n$ is a disturbance vector, and $F(\bullet)$ is a smooth vector field with $f_i(\bullet)$ being its entries; hence (3.25) can be rewritten as:

$$x(k) = \begin{bmatrix} x_1(k) & \ldots & x_i(k) & \ldots & x_n(k) \end{bmatrix}^\top,$$
$$d(k) = \begin{bmatrix} d_1(k) & \ldots & d_i(k) & \ldots & d_n(k) \end{bmatrix}^\top,$$

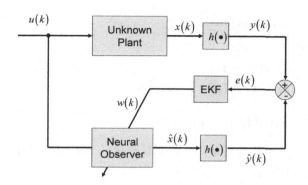

FIGURE 3.4 Neural observer scheme for nonlinear output.

$$x_i\,(k+1) = f_i\,(x\,(k)\,,u\,(k)) + d_i\,(k)\,, \quad i = 1,\dots,n,$$
$$y\,(k) = h\,(x\,(k))\,. \tag{3.26}$$

For system (3.25), we propose a recurrent neural Luenberger type observer (RHONO) with the following structure:

$$\widehat{x}\,(k) = \left[\; \widehat{x}_1\,(k) \quad \dots \quad \widehat{x}_i\,(k) \quad \dots \quad \widehat{x}_n\,(k) \;\right]^{\top},$$
$$\widehat{x}_i(k+1) = w_i^{\top} z_i(\widehat{x}(k), u(k)) + g_i e\,(k)\,,$$
$$\widehat{y}\,(k) = h\,(\widehat{x}\,(k))\,, \quad i = 1,\dots,n, \tag{3.27}$$

with $g_i \in \Re^p$ and $z_i(x(k), u(k))$ as defined in (2.7). The proposed neural observer scheme is shown in Fig. 3.4.

Then, considering (3.25)–(3.27) it is possible to extend Theorem 3.1 for an unknown nonlinear system with nonlinear output as follows:

Theorem 3.2. *For system (3.26), the RHONO (3.27), trained with the EKF-based algorithm (3.8), ensures that the ith $(i = 1, 2, \dots, n)$ estimation error (3.11) and the output error (3.10) are semi-globally uniformly ultimately bounded (SGUUB); moreover, the RHONO weights remain bounded.*

Proof. Since $h\,(\bullet)$ is a known output function, which is Lipschitz in $x\,(k)$,

$$e\,(k) = y\,(k) - \widehat{y}\,(k)$$
$$= h\,(x\,(k)) - h\,(\widehat{x}\,(k))\,,$$
$$\|h\,(x\,(k)) - h\,(\widehat{x}\,(k))\| \le L\,\|x\,(k) - \widehat{x}\,(k)\| \tag{3.28}$$

with L being the Lipschitz constant [3]. First, consider the candidate Lyapunov function

$$V_i\,(k) = \widetilde{w}_i^T\,(k)\,P_i\,(k)\,\widetilde{w}_i\,(k) + \widetilde{x}_i^T\,(k)\,\widetilde{x}_i\,(k) \tag{3.29}$$

whose first increment is defined as

$$\Delta V_i(k) = V_i(k+1) - V_i(k)$$
$$= \widetilde{w}_i^T(k+1) P_i(k+1) \widetilde{w}_i(k+1) + \widetilde{x}_i^T(k+1) \widetilde{x}_i(k+1)$$
$$- \widetilde{w}_i^T(k) P_i(k) \widetilde{w}_i(k) - \widetilde{x}_i^T(k) \widetilde{x}_i(k). \tag{3.30}$$

Substituting (3.10) and (3.11) into (3.30) gives

$$\Delta V_i(k) = \left[\widetilde{w}_i(k) - \eta_i K_i(k) e(k)\right]^T [A_i(k)] \left[\widetilde{w}_i(k) - \eta_i K_i(k) e(k)\right]$$
$$+ \left[f_i(k) - g_i e(k)\right]^T \left[f_i(k) - g_i e(k)\right]$$
$$- \widetilde{w}_i^T(k) P_i(k) \widetilde{w}_i(k) - \widetilde{x}_i^T(k) \widetilde{x}_i(k)$$
$$= -\widetilde{w}_i^T(k) B_i(k) \widetilde{w}_i(k) - \eta_i e^T(k) K_i^T(k) A_i(k) \widetilde{w}_i(k)$$
$$- \eta_i \widetilde{w}_i^T(k) A_i(k) e(k) + \eta_i^2 e^T(k) K_i^T(k) A_i(k) K_i(k) e(k)$$
$$+ f_i^T(k) f_i(k) - f_i^T(k) g_i e(k) - e^T(k) g_i^T f_i(k)$$
$$+ e^T(k) g_i^T g_i e(k) - \widetilde{x}_i^T(k) \widetilde{x}_i(k) \tag{3.31}$$

with

$$A_i(k) = P_i(k) - B_i(k),$$
$$B_i(k) = K_i(k) H_i^T(k) P_i(k) + Q_i(k),$$
$$f_i(k) = \widetilde{w}_i^T(k) z_i(\widehat{x}(k), u(k)) + \epsilon'_{z_i}.$$

Using the following inequalities;

$$X^T X + Y^T Y \geq -X^T Y - Y^T X,$$
$$-\lambda_{\min}(P) X^2 \geq -X^T P X \geq -\lambda_{\max}(P) X^2,$$

which are valid $\forall X, Y \in \Re^n$, $\forall P \in \Re^{n \times n}$, $P = P^T > 0$, and replacing (3.28) in (3.31), we obtain

$$\Delta V_i(k) \leq -\|\widetilde{w}_i(k)\|^2 \lambda_{\min}(B_i(k)) + 2\|f_i(k)\|^2$$
$$+ \eta_i^2 \|\widetilde{x}(k)\|^2 \|L\|^2 \|K_i(k)\|^2 \lambda_{\max} A_i(k)$$
$$+ 2\|\widetilde{x}(k)\|^2 \|L\|^2 \|g_i\|^2 - \|\widetilde{x}(k)\|^2$$
$$+ \|K_i(k)\|^2 \|A_i(k)\|^2 \|\widetilde{w}_i(k)\|^2 + \eta_i^2 \|\widetilde{x}(k)\|^2 \|L\|^2. \tag{3.32}$$

Replacing $f_i(k)$ in (3.32) yields

$$\Delta V_i(k) \leq -\|\widetilde{w}_i(k)\|^2 \lambda_{\min}(B_i(k)) + 2\|\widetilde{w}_i(k)\|^2 \|z_i(\widehat{x}(k), u(k))\|^2$$
$$+ \eta_i^2 \|\widetilde{x}(k)\|^2 \|L\|^2 \|K_i(k)\|^2 \lambda_{\max} A_i(k)$$
$$+ 2\|\widetilde{x}(k)\|^2 \|L\|^2 \|g_i\|^2 - \|\widetilde{x}(k)\|^2 + \eta_i^2 \|\widetilde{x}(k)\|^2 \|L\|^2$$
$$+ \|K_i(k)\|^2 \|A_i(k)\|^2 \|\widetilde{w}_i(k)\|^2 + 2\left|\epsilon'_{z_i}\right|^2. \tag{3.33}$$

Defining

$$E_i(k) = \lambda_{\min}(B_i(k)) - \|K_i(k)\|^2 \|A_i(k)\|^2 - 2\|z_i(\widehat{x}(k), u(k))\|^2, \qquad (3.34)$$

$$F_i(k) = 1 - \eta_i^2 \|L\|^2 \|K_i(k)\|^2 \lambda_{\max} A_i(k) - 2\|L\|^2 \|g_i\|^2 - \eta_i^2 \|L\|^2, \qquad (3.35)$$

one can express (3.33) as

$$\Delta V_i(k) \le -\|\widetilde{w}_i(k)\|^2 E_i(k) - \|\widetilde{x}(k)\|^2 F_i(k) + 2\left|\epsilon'_{z_i}\right|^2.$$

Hence, $\Delta V_i(k) < 0$, whenever

$$\|\widetilde{x}(k)\|^2 > \sqrt{\frac{2\left|\epsilon'_{z_i}\right|^2}{F_i(k)}} \equiv \kappa_1(k),$$

or

$$\|\widetilde{w}_i(k)\|^2 > \sqrt{\frac{2\left|\epsilon'_{z_i}\right|^2}{E_i(k)}} \equiv \kappa_2(k).$$

Therefore, the solution of (3.10) and (3.11) is stable; hence the estimation error and the RHONN weights are SGUUB. Now, to proceed with the proof, consider the Lyapunov function candidate

$$V_i(k) = \sum_{i=1}^{n} (\widetilde{w}_i(k) P_i(k) \widetilde{w}_i(k) + \widetilde{x}_i(k) \widetilde{x}_i(k)) \qquad (3.36)$$

with

$$\begin{aligned}
\Delta V_i(k) = \sum_{i=1}^{n} & (\widetilde{w}_i(k+1) P_i(k+1) \widetilde{w}_i(k+1) \\
& + \widetilde{x}_i(k+1) \widetilde{x}_i(k+1) \\
& - \widetilde{w}_i(k) P_i(k) \widetilde{w}_i(k) \\
& - \widetilde{x}_i(k) P_i(k) \widetilde{x}_i(k)).
\end{aligned} \qquad (3.37)$$

Therefore, as above, (3.36) can be expressed as

$$\Delta V_i(k) \le \sum_{i=1}^{n} \left(-\|\widetilde{w}_i(k)\|^2 E_i(k) - \|\widetilde{x}(k)\|^2 F_i(k) + 2\left|\epsilon'_{z_i}\right|^2 \right)$$

with $E_i(k)$ and $F_i(k)$ as in (3.34) and (3.35), respectively. As a result, $\Delta V_i(k) < 0$ whenever

$$\|\widetilde{x}(k)\| > \kappa_1(k)$$

or

$$\|\widetilde{w}_i(k)\| > \kappa_2(k),$$

and if $\|\widetilde{x}(k)\| > \kappa_1(k)$ and $\|\widetilde{w}_i(k)\| > \kappa_2(k)$, $\forall i = 1, \ldots, n$ holds, then $\Delta V_i(k) < 0$.

Finally, considering (3.28), it is easy too see that the output error has an algebraic relation with $\tilde{x}(k)$; for that reason, if $\tilde{x}(k)$ is bounded $e(k)$ is bounded, too:

$$e(k) = h(x(k)) - h(\widehat{x}(k)),$$
$$\|e(k)\| = \|h(x(k)) - h(\widehat{x}(k))\| \leq L \|\tilde{x}(k)\|. \qquad \square$$

3.3 APPLICATIONS

3.3.1 Human Immunodeficiency Virus (HIV)

Measurements in biomedical systems are very expensive, difficult, and sometimes impossible to achieve. State estimation by neural networks could be important in providing clinicians with a better understanding of the immune markers in patients with viral infectious diseases. Among different classes of infectious diseases during the last 30 years, HIV has been extensively studied, due to the fact that HIV can lead to the acquired immunodeficiency syndrome (AIDS). According to statistics in the global summary of the AIDS epidemic from the World Health Organization (WHO) [42], by the end of 2007, estimated 33 million people were living with HIV worldwide. That same year, approximately 2 million died of AIDS. However, there is currently no known cure to tackle the infection. Clinicians need more information about the infection in patients; hence the need for novel tools to provide immune function markers in patients with HIV [43]. Observers in HIV infection have been a growing area [34,35,43–49]. The majority of these works have considered continuous-time measurements; nevertheless, such measurements are performed only a few times per year. Moreover, the requirement of the model for the observer design is a drawback in these approaches. Therefore, in this application we use the proposed RHONO to estimate both, a model for the system and the state variables measurement.

3.3.1.1 HIV Model

In this section, the neural observer is applied to an HIV model. The HIV model [31,32] includes the concentration of infected (T^i) and uninfected (T) cells, together with the number of viral cells in the blood stream (V). Using the Euler method, the HIV model [31,32] can be represented in discrete-time as:

$$T(k+1) = T(k) + \delta s(k) - \delta \mu_T T(k)$$
$$+ \delta r \frac{T(k)V(k)}{C+V(k)} - \delta \xi(k) k_v T(k) V(k),$$
$$T^i(k+1) = T^i(k) + \delta \xi(k) k_v T(k) V(k)$$
$$- \delta \mu_T^i T^i(k) - \delta r \frac{T^i(k)V(k)}{C+V(k)},$$
$$V(k+1) = V(k) + \delta Nr \frac{T^i(k)V(k)}{C+V(k)}$$

$$-\delta k_T T(k) V(k) + \delta g_v \frac{V(k)}{c + V(k)},$$

$$y(k) = h\left(T(k), T^i(k), V(k)\right) \tag{3.38}$$

where $s(t)$ is the source of new CD4 cells produced by the Timo; μ_T is the death speed of the uninfected CD4; μ_T^i is the death speed of the infected cells; k_v is the speed of the uninfected cells becoming cells with virus; k_T is the speed of lymphocytes CD8 eliminating the virus; r is the maximum proliferation of the CD4 cells population; N is the number of free viruses produced by the infected cells; C is the semi-constant of the proliferation process; c is the total daily drug dosage in chemotherapy; b is the half-constant saturation value of an external source of virus; g_v is the level under which other cells (that are not lymphocytes) are free of the virus in the blood, h is the output matrix, given by $h = \begin{bmatrix} 1 & 1 & 0 \end{bmatrix}^\top$, and δ is the sampling period.

3.3.1.2 RHONO for the HIV Model

In this section the discrete-time RHONO for unknown nonlinear systems with linear output is designed to estimate the model dynamics and state measurements for an HIV model [33–35].

The RHONO is applied to HIV dynamics, whose nonlinear dynamics is considered unknown. To estimate the state, which is defined by the number of viral cells in the blood torrent ($V = x_3$), the online concentration of infected cells ($T^i = x_2$), and the online concentration of uninfected cells ($T = x_1$). For this case T^i and T measurements are considered known, then $y(k) = \begin{bmatrix} x_1(k) & x_2(k) \end{bmatrix}^\top$; we use a sampling time of 20 minutes. The neural dynamic used for this state estimation is given by

$$\begin{aligned}
\widehat{x}_1(k+1) &= w_{11}(k) S(\widehat{x}_3(k)) \\
&\quad + w_{12}(k) S(\widehat{x}_1(k))^2 S(\widehat{x}_2(k)) \\
&\quad + w_{13}(k) S(\widehat{x}_1(k)) S(\widehat{x}_3(k)) S(u(k)) \\
&\quad + w_{14}(k) S(\widehat{x}_1(k)) S(\widehat{x}_2(k)) + g_1 e(k), \\
\widehat{x}_2(k+1) &= w_{21}(k) \widehat{x}_1(k) \widehat{x}_3(k) + w_{22}(k) \widehat{x}_2(k) \\
&\quad + w_{23}(k) S(\widehat{x}_3(k)) S(u(k)) \widehat{x}_2(k) \widehat{x}_3(k) \\
&\quad + g_2 e(k), \\
\widehat{x}_3(k+1) &= w_{31}(k) S(\widehat{x}_2(k)) S(\widehat{x}_3(k)) S(u(k)) \\
&\quad + w_{32}(k) S(\widehat{x}_1(k)) S(\widehat{x}_3(k)) \\
&\quad + w_{33}(k) S(\widehat{x}_1(k)) S(\widehat{x}_3(k))^2 + g_2 e(k), \\
\widehat{y}(k) &= \begin{bmatrix} \widehat{x}_1(k) & \widehat{x}_2(k) \end{bmatrix}^\top
\end{aligned} \tag{3.39}$$

where $\widehat{x}_1$, $\widehat{x}_2$, and $\widehat{x}_3$ are the estimates of concentration of uninfected cells (T), concentration of infected cells (T^i), and the number of viral cells in the blood stream (V), respectively. The input $u(k) = c$ is the total daily drug dosage in

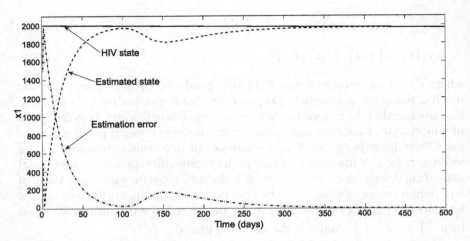

FIGURE 3.5 Time evolution of the state $x_1(k)$ (solid line), its estimated $\widehat{x}_1(k)$ (dashed line) and the estimation error $\widetilde{x}_1(k)$ (dashed–dotted line).

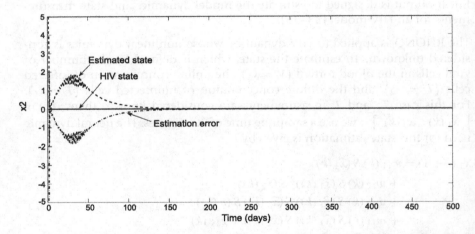

FIGURE 3.6 Time evolution of the state $x_2(k)$ (solid line), its estimated $\widehat{x}_2(k)$ (dashed line) and the estimation error $\widetilde{x}_2(k)$ (dashed–dotted line).

chemotherapy. The training is performed online, using a parallel configuration as displayed in Fig. 3.1. All the NN states are initialized in a random way. The associated covariance matrices are initialized as diagonals, and the nonzero elements are: $P_1(0) = P_2(0) = P_3(0) = 100{,}000$, $Q_1(0) = Q_2(0) = Q_3(0) = 1000$, and $R_1(0) = R_2(0) = R_3(0) = 1000$, respectively, and the Luenberger parameter vector is $g = \begin{bmatrix} 0.05 & 0.01 & 1.07 \end{bmatrix}^T$. The simulation results are presented in Figs. 3.5, 3.6, and 3.7. They display the time evolution of the

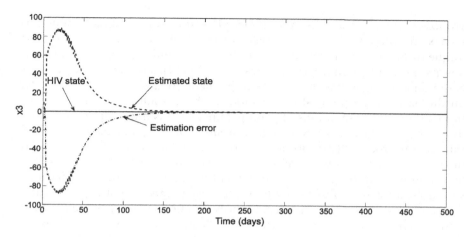

FIGURE 3.7 Time evolution of the state $x_3(k)$ (solid line), its estimated $\widehat{x}_3(k)$ (dashed line) and the estimation error $\widetilde{x}_3(k)$ (dashed–dotted line).

estimated states $x_1(k)$, $x_2(k)$, and $x_3(k)$ including their estimation errors, respectively.

3.3.2 Rotatory Induction Motor

In this section, we present the RHONO proposed in Section 3.1 of this chapter, as applied to a three-phase induction motor, which is one of the most used actuators for industrial applications due to its reliability, ruggedness, and relatively low cost. Modeling of an induction motor is challenging, since its dynamics is described by a multivariate, coupled, and highly nonlinear system [5,6]. A well-known problem, for induction motor applications, is that electrical parameters might not be accurately known, or might significantly vary when the motor is operating, which has motivated various approaches for their identification [7–10]. Among the wide range of available contributions in this direction, one can find results for the estimation of a limited number of required electrical parameters, under different assumptions [7–10]. Traditionally, induction motor control is performed in steady state for constant speed profiles [9,10]; however, for many applications such as electric vehicle, mass transportation, advanced drilling, and steel milling operation, among others, it is necessary to track time-varying reference signals. Therefore recent works on control of induction motors are focused on the field oriented control (FOC) [11], exact input–output linearization, adaptive input output linearization, and direct torque control (DTC) ([11] and references therein). Robustness of those controllers significantly depends on accurate knowledge of the system states. In practice, fluxes are not easily measurable, therefore an observer is needed to estimate them [12]. Besides, most of those works were developed for a continuous-time model of the motor. In [6], a discrete-time model is proposed, as well as an observer. In [13,14] and in [6], continuous-time observers are studied. All these observers assume that the parameters and load torque of the motor model are known. In [12,13] and [15], continuous-time observers for induction motor are considered; in [14], a discrete-time observer based on linearization is proposed. All the mentioned observers are designed on the basis of the physical motor model, which results in a sensitive control with respect to variations of plant parameters. It is important to note that the proposed scheme is developed assuming that the plant parameters and external disturbances (load torque) are unknown. Furthermore, the proposed methodology can deal with well-known uncertainties, namely rotor parameter variations with frequency due to skin effect, other nonlinear imperfections such as heating, main flux path saturation, leakage variation or flux migration due to rotor skew and external disturbances variations [16,17], as well as load torque changes, without any previous knowledge of their dynamics. Most of these phenomena are presented during induction motor operation [11].

3.3.2.1 Model Description

The sixth-order discrete-time induction motor model in the stator fixed reference frame (α, β), under the assumptions of equal mutual inductances and linear magnetic circuit, is given by [6]

$$
\begin{aligned}
\omega\,(k+1) &= \omega\,(k) + \frac{\mu}{\alpha}\,(1-\alpha) \\
&\quad \times M\left(i^{\beta}\,(k)\,\psi^{\alpha}\,(k) - i^{\alpha}\,(k)\,\psi^{\beta}\,(k)\right) \\
&\quad - \left(\frac{T}{J}\right) T_L\,(k),
\end{aligned}
$$

$$
\begin{aligned}
\psi^{\alpha}\,(k+1) &= \cos\left(n_p\theta\,(k+1)\right)\rho_1\,(k) \\
&\quad - \sin\left(n_p\theta\,(k+1)\right)\rho_2\,(k),
\end{aligned}
$$

$$
\begin{aligned}
\psi^{\beta}\,(k+1) &= \sin\left(n_p\theta\,(k+1)\right)\rho_1\,(k) \\
&\quad + \cos\left(n_p\theta\,(k+1)\right)\rho_2\,(k),
\end{aligned}
$$

$$
i^{\alpha}\,(k+1) = \varphi^{\alpha}\,(k) + \frac{T}{\sigma}u^{\alpha}\,(k),
$$

$$
i^{\beta}\,(k+1) = \varphi^{\beta}\,(k) + \frac{T}{\sigma}u^{\beta}\,(k),
$$

$$
\begin{aligned}
\theta\,(k+1) &= \theta\,(k) + \omega\,(k)\,T + \frac{\mu}{\alpha}\left[T - \frac{(1-a)}{\alpha}\right] \\
&\quad \times M\left(i^{\beta}\,(k)\,\psi^{\alpha}\,(k) - i^{\alpha}\,(k)\,\psi^{\beta}\,(k)\right) \\
&\quad - \frac{T_L\,(k)}{J}T^2,
\end{aligned}
\tag{3.40}
$$

with

$$
\begin{aligned}
\rho_1\,(k) &= a\left(\cos\left(\phi\,(k)\right)\psi^{\alpha}\,(k) + \sin\left(\phi\,(k)\right)\psi^{\beta}\,(k)\right) \\
&\quad + b\left(\cos\left(\phi\,(k)\right)i^{\alpha}\,(k) + \sin\left(\phi\,(k)\right)i^{\beta}\,(k)\right),
\end{aligned}
$$

$$\rho_2(k) = a\left(\cos\left(\phi(k)\right)\psi^\alpha(k) - \sin\left(\phi(k)\right)\psi^\beta(k)\right)$$
$$+ b\left(\cos\left(\phi(k)\right)i^\alpha(k) - \sin\left(\phi(k)\right)i^\beta(k)\right),$$
$$\varphi^\alpha(k) = i^\alpha(k) + \alpha\beta T\psi^\alpha(k) + n_p\beta T\omega(k)\psi^\alpha(k)$$
$$- \gamma T i^\alpha(k),$$
$$\varphi^\beta(k) = i^\beta(k) + \alpha\beta T\psi^\beta(k) + n_p\beta T\omega(k)\psi^\beta(k)$$
$$- \gamma T i^\beta(k),$$
$$\phi(k) = n_p\theta(k),$$

with $b = (1-a)M$, $\alpha = \frac{R_r}{L_r}$, $\gamma = \frac{M^2 R_r}{\sigma L_r^2} + \frac{R_s}{\sigma}$, $\sigma = L_s - \frac{M^2}{L_r}$, $\beta = \frac{M}{\sigma L_r}$, $a = e^{-\alpha T}$, and $\mu = \frac{M n_p}{J L_r}$ where L_s, L_r, and M are the stator, rotor and mutual inductance respectively; R_s and R_r are the stator and rotor resistances, respectively; n_p is the number of pole pairs; T is the time sample period; T_L is the load torque; i^α and i^β represent the currents in the α and β phases, respectively; ψ^α and ψ^β represent the fluxes in the α and β phases, respectively; u^α and u^β represent the input voltages in the α and β phases, respectively, and θ is the rotor angular displacement.

3.3.2.2 *Neural Observer Design*

We apply the RHONO (Fig. 3.1), developed in Section 3.1, to estimate the state of a three-phase induction motor (3.40). Simulations are performed for the system (3.40), using the following parameters: $R_s = 14\ \Omega$; $L_s = 400$ mH; $M = 377$ mH; $R_r = 10.1\ \Omega$; $L_r = 412.8$ mH; $n_p = 2$; $J = 0.01$ kg m^2; $T = 0.0001$ s. To estimate the state of system (3.40), we use the RHONO, presented in Section 3.1, with $n = 6$ trained with the EKF:

$$\hat{x}_1(k+1) = w_{11}(k)S(\hat{x}_1(k)) + w_{12}(k)S(\hat{x}_1)S(\hat{x}_3(k))\hat{x}_4(k)$$
$$+ w_{13}(k)S(\hat{x}_1)S(\hat{x}_2(k))\hat{x}_5(k) + g_1 e(k),$$
$$\hat{x}_2(k+1) = w_{21}(k)S(\hat{x}_1(k))S(\hat{x}_3(k)) + w_{22}(k)\hat{x}_5(k) + g_2 e(k),$$
$$\hat{x}_3(k+1) = w_{31}(k)S(\hat{x}_1(k))S(\hat{x}_2(k)) + w_{32}(k)\hat{x}_4(k) + g_3 e(k),$$
$$\hat{x}_4(k+1) = w_{41}(k)S(\hat{x}_2(k)) + w_{42}(k)S(\hat{x}_3(k)) + w_{43}(k)S(\hat{x}_4(k))$$
$$+ w_{44}(k)u^\alpha(k) + g_4 e(k),$$
$$\hat{x}_5(k+1) = w_{51}(k)S(\hat{x}_2(k)) + w_{52}(k)S(\hat{x}_3(k)) + w_{53}(k)S(\hat{x}_5(k))$$
$$+ w_{54}(k)u^\beta(k) + g_5 e(k),$$
$$\hat{x}_6(k+1) = w_{61}(k)S(\hat{x}_2(k)) + w_{62}(k)S(\hat{x}_3(k)) + w_{63}(k)S(\hat{x}_6(k))$$
$$+ g_6 e(k), \tag{3.41}$$

where $\hat{x}_1$ estimates the angular speed ω; $\hat{x}_2$ and $\hat{x}_3$ estimate the fluxes ψ^α and ψ^β, respectively; $\hat{x}_4$ and $\hat{x}_5$ estimate the currents i^α and i^β, respectively; finally, $\hat{x}_6$ estimates the angular displacement θ. The inputs u^α and u^β are selected as chirp functions.

The training is performed online, using a parallel configuration. All the NN states are initialized in a random way. The associated covariance matrices

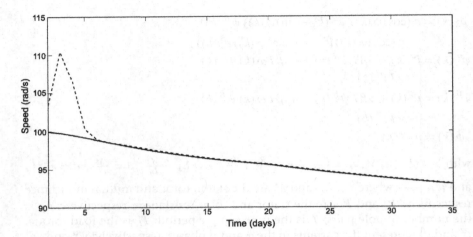

FIGURE 3.8 Angular speed ω (solid line) and its estimated $\widehat{x}_1$ (dashed line).

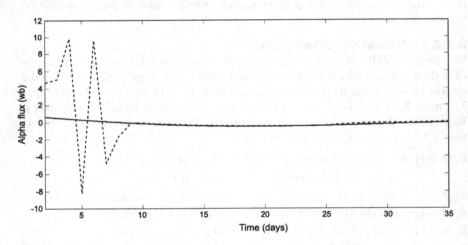

FIGURE 3.9 Alpha flux ψ^{α} (solid line) and its estimated $\widehat{x}_2$ (dashed line).

are initialized as diagonals, and the nonzero elements are: $P_i(0) = 10,000$, $Q_i(0) = 500$, and $R_i(0) = 10,000$ $(i = 1, \ldots, 6)$, respectively. The simulation results are presented in Figs. 3.8–3.13; they display the time evolution of the estimated states $\widehat{x}_i(k)$ $(i = 1, \ldots, 6)$, respectively. Figs. 3.14 and 3.15 portray the load torque applied as an external disturbance and the parametric variation introduced in the rotor resistance (R_r) as a variation of 1 Ohm per second, respectively. This neural network structure is determined heuristically in order to minimize the state estimation error; however, it has a block control form [5] in order to ease the synthesis of nonlinear controllers [1].

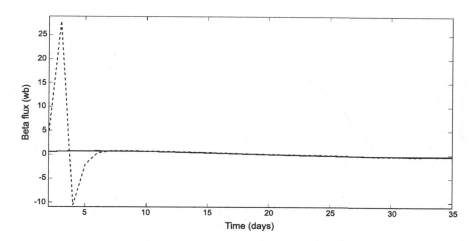

FIGURE 3.10 Beta flux ψ^β (solid line) and its estimate $\widehat{x}_3$ (dashed line).

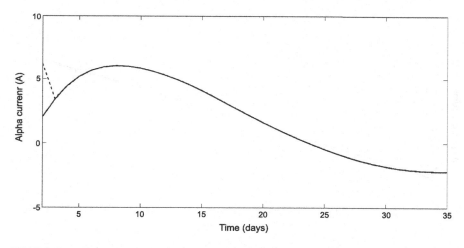

FIGURE 3.11 Alpha current i^α (solid line) and its estimate $\widehat{x}_4$ (dashed line).

It is important to note that for induction motor applications, it is unusual to use chirp signals (sine wave signal whose frequency increases at a linear rate with respect to time) as inputs [1]. In this paper, they are used for the purpose of state estimation to excite most of the plant dynamics. For modeling of nonlinear system structures, it is important to represent a wide range of frequencies. Input signals attempting to meet this demand include pseudo-random binary sequences (PRBS), random Gaussian noise, and chirp signals (swept sinusoid). All of these input signals have advantages which include independent noise estimation and reduction of data sets, among others; how-

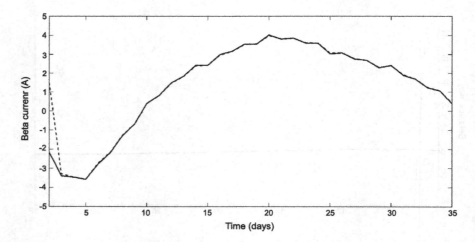

FIGURE 3.12 Beta current i^β (solid line) and its estimate $\hat{x}_5$ (dashed line).

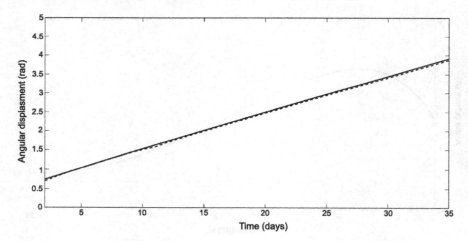

FIGURE 3.13 Angular displacement θ (solid line) and its estimate $\hat{x}_6$ (dashed line).

ever, chirp signals have been generally found to provide more consistent results and have been used successfully in the past for modeling the dynamics of complex nonlinear systems. For supplementary information, see also [18–20].

3.3.2.3 Real-Time Results

The experiments are performed using a benchmark, which includes a PC for supervising, a PWM unit for the power stage, a dSPACE DS1104 board (dSPACE is a registered trademark of dSPACE GmbH, Germany) for data acquisition and control of the system, and a three-phase induction motor as the plant to be controlled, with the following characteristics: 220 V, 60 Hz, 0.19 kW,

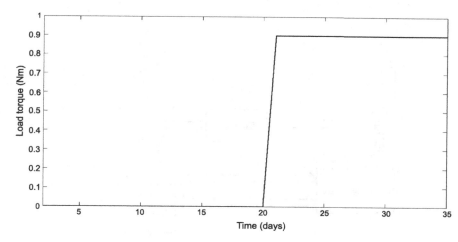

FIGURE 3.14 Load Torque (T_L).

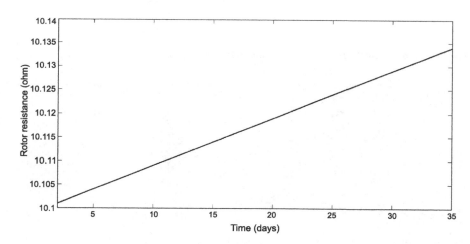

FIGURE 3.15 Rotor resistance variation (R_r).

1660 rpm, and 1.3 A [1]. Pictures and a scheme of the benchmark are included as follows: Fig. 3.16 presents a schematic representation of the benchmark used for experiments. Fig. 3.17 displays a view of the PC and the DS1104 board and the PWM driver. The DS1104 board allows downloading applications directly from Simulink (Matlab and Simulink are registered trademarks of MathWorks Inc., USA). The experiment implemented on this benchmark uses the Neural Network State Estimation discussed in Section 3.3; the experiment is performed with a constant load torque applied as an inertial load coupled to the induction motor as shown in Fig. 3.18.

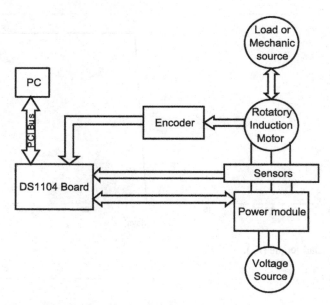

FIGURE 3.16 Schematic representation of the control prototype.

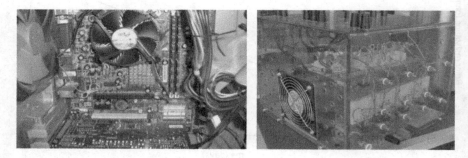

FIGURE 3.17 PC with DS1104 board and PWM driver.

FIGURE 3.18 Induction motor coupled with the load and the encoder.

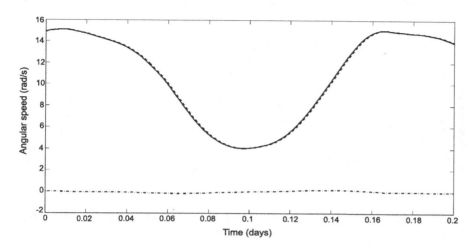

FIGURE 3.19 Real-time rotor speed estimation (plant signal in solid line and neural signal in dashed line).

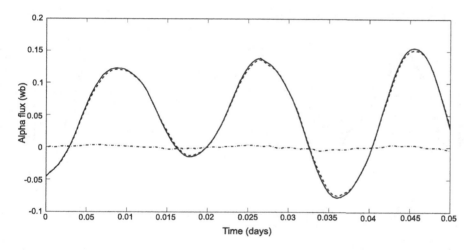

FIGURE 3.20 Real-time alpha flux estimation (plant signal (solid line) and neural signal (dashed line)).

During the estimation process the plant and the NN operate in open-loop. Both of them (plant and NN) have the same input vector $\begin{bmatrix} u_\alpha & u_\beta \end{bmatrix}^\top$; u_α and u_β are chirp functions, with 200 volts of amplitude and incremental frequencies from 0 to 150 Hz and from 0 to 200 Hz, respectively. The implementation is performed with a sampling time of 0.0005 s. The results of the real-time implementation are presented as follows: Fig. 3.19 displays the estimation performance for the speed rotor; Fig. 3.20 and Fig. 3.21 present the estima-

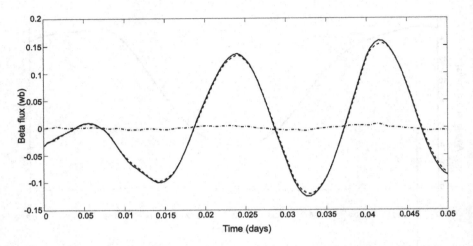

FIGURE 3.21 Real-time beta flux estimation (plant signal (solid line) and neural signal (dashed line)).

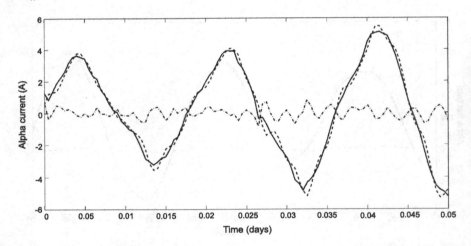

FIGURE 3.22 Real-time alpha current estimation (plant signal (solid line) and neural signal (dashed line)).

tion performance for the fluxes in phase α and β, respectively. Fig. 3.22 and Fig. 3.23 portray the estimation performance for currents in phase α and β, respectively. Finally, Table 3.1 presents the standard deviation for the state estimation errors.

It is worth to mention that, in this case, for real-time state estimation, there is no delay. In fact, all required calculations are performed in between consecutive samples. Considering that the induction motor is working in open loop,

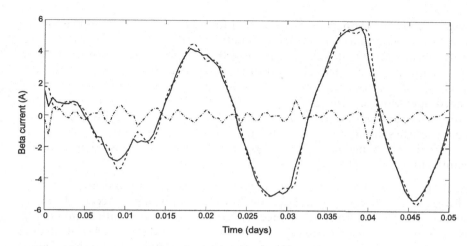

FIGURE 3.23 Real-time beta current estimation (plant signal (solid line) and neural signal (dashed line)).

Table 3.1 Standard deviation and mean value for the state estimation error

Variable	Standard Deviation	Mean Value
$\omega - \widehat{x}_1$	0.0995 rad/s	-1.6478×10^{-4} rad/s
$\psi^\alpha - \widehat{x}_2$	0.0028 wb	3.0836×10^{-4} wb
$\psi^\beta - \widehat{x}_3$	0.0026 wb	-3.9090×10^{-4} wb
$i^\alpha - \widehat{x}_4$	0.0332 A	-7.0384×10^{-4} A
$i^\beta - \widehat{x}_5$	0.0381 A	-2.9987×10^{-4} A

there is no effect of the RHONN structure on its performance. It is important to remark that the state estimation proposed in this chapter is performed using a chirp signal in order to excite most of the plant dynamics as is shown in Figs. 3.19–3.23. Due to the use of this signal, neither the speed nor the flux settle to nominal values. The included real-time results illustrate the effectiveness of the proposed neural observer, as applied to an electric three-phase squirrel cage induction motor, without knowledge or estimation of the parameters, under the presence of parametric variations caused by winding heating due to motor operation.

3.3.3 Linear Induction Motor

In this section, we apply the RHONO proposed in Section 3.1 as applied to a three-phase linear induction motor (LIM). Linear induction motor is a special electrical machine, in which the electrical energy is converted directly into mechanical energy of translatory motion. Strong interest in these machines arose in the early 1970s. In the late 1970s, the research intensity and number of publications dropped. After 1980, LIM found their first noticeable applications in transportation, industry, automation, and home appliances„ among other things [21,22]. LIM has many excellent performance features such as high-starting thrust force, elimination of gears between motor and motion devices, reduction of mechanical loses and the size of motion devices, high speed operation, silence, and so on [22,23]. The driving principles of the LIM are similar to the traditional rotary induction motor (RIM), but its control characteristics are more complicated than those of the RIM, and the parameters are time-varying due to the change of operating conditions, such as speed, temperature, and rail configuration.

The idea of using linear motors for mass public transportation is not new [24]. However, the attention is focused on the LIM again due to recent developments of large smart grids. The modern electric power grid with wind energy is a complex adaptive system under semi-autonomous distributed control, due to its high complexity and the presence of unknown uncertainties and disturbances [25]. The integration of plug-in hybrid and electric vehicles means that the control problem of power grids can be very difficult to handle with traditional approaches, requiring the application of intelligent control approaches. For example, charging a large number of electric vehicles randomly or simultaneously without an intelligent infrastructure will increase the load on the electric grid, causing adverse effects and an increase in cost of electric vehicle usage. Intelligent scheduling of vehicles for charging and dynamic load forecasting will become of vital importance. On the other hand, electric vehicles with the use of gridable vehicles, information technology and advanced computational methods can make the electric grid efficient, reliable, distributed, clean, and interoperable [25].

3.3.3.1 Model Description

In this section, the proposed RHONO of Section 3.1 is applied to the α–β model of an LIM discretized by the Euler technique [6,26,27] as follows:

$$
\begin{aligned}
q_m(k+1) &= q_m(k) + v(k)T, \\
v(k+1) &= (1 - K_2 T)v(k) - k_1 T \lambda_{r\alpha}(k)\rho_1 i_{s\alpha}(k) \\
&\quad - k_1 T \lambda_{r\beta}(k)\rho_2 i_{s\alpha}(k) \\
&\quad + k_1 T \lambda_{r\alpha}(k)\rho_2 i_{s\beta}(k) \\
&\quad - k_1 T \lambda_{r\beta}(k)\rho_1 i_{s\beta}(k) - k_3 T F_L, \\
\lambda_{r\alpha}(k+1) &= (1 - k_6 T)\lambda_{r\alpha}(k) + k_4 T v(k)\rho_1 i_{s\alpha}(k) \\
&\quad - k_4 T \rho_1 i_{s\alpha}(k) + k_5 T \rho_2 i_{s\alpha}(k) \\
&\quad + k_4 T \rho_2 i_{s\beta}(k) - k_4 T v(k)\rho_2 i_{s\beta}(k) \\
&\quad + k_5 T \rho_1 i_{s\beta}(k), \\
\lambda_{r\beta}(k+1) &= (1 - k_6 T)\lambda_{r\beta}(k) + k_4 T v(k)\rho_2 i_{s\alpha}(k) \\
&\quad - k_4 T \rho_2 i_{s\alpha}(k) - k_5 T \rho_1 i_{s\alpha}(k) \\
&\quad + k_4 T \rho_1 i_{s\beta}(k) + k_4 T v(k)\rho_1 i_{s\beta}(k)
\end{aligned}
$$

$$+ k_5 T \rho_2 i_{s\beta}(k),$$
$$i_{s\alpha}(k+1) = (1 + k_9 T) i_{s\alpha}(k) - k_7 T \lambda_{r\alpha}(k) \rho_2$$
$$- k_8 T \lambda_{r\alpha}(k) v(k) \rho_1 + k_7 T \lambda_{r\beta}(k) \rho_1$$
$$- k_8 T \lambda_{r\beta}(k) v(k) \rho_2 - k_{10} T u_\alpha(k),$$
$$i_{s\beta}(k+1) = (1 + k_9 T) i_{s\beta}(k) + k_8 T \lambda_{r\alpha}(k) v(k) \rho_2$$
$$- k_7 T \lambda_{r\alpha}(k) \rho_1 - k_7 T \lambda_{r\beta}(k) \rho_2$$
$$- k_8 T \lambda_{r\beta}(k) v(k) \rho_1 - k_{10} T u_\beta(k), \tag{3.42}$$

with

$$\rho_1 = \sin(n_p q_m(k)),$$
$$\rho_2 = \cos(n_p q_m(k)),$$
$$k_1 = \frac{n_p L_{sr}}{D_m L_r},$$
$$k_2 = \frac{R_m}{D_m},$$
$$k_3 = \frac{1}{D_m},$$
$$k_4 = n_p L_{sr},$$
$$k_5 = \frac{R_r L_{sr}}{L_r},$$
$$k_6 = \frac{R_r}{L_r},$$
$$k_7 = \frac{L_{sr} R_r}{L_r (L_{sr}^2 - L_s L_r)},$$
$$k_8 = \frac{L_{sr} n_p}{L_{sr}^2 - L_s L_r},$$
$$k_9 = \frac{L_r^2 R_s + L_{sr}^2 R_r}{L_r (L_{sr}^2 - L_s L_r)},$$
$$k_{10} = \frac{L_r}{L_{sr}^2 - L_s L_r},$$

where $q_m(k)$ is the position, $v(k)$ is the linear velocity, $\lambda_{r\alpha}(k)$ and $\lambda_{r\beta}(k)$ are the α-axis and β-axis secondary fluxes, respectively, $i_{s\alpha}(k)$ and $i_{s\beta}(k)$ are the α-axis and β-axis primary currents, respectively, $u_{s\alpha}(k)$ and $u_{s\beta}(k)$ are the α-axis and β-axis primary voltages, R_s is the winding resistance per phase, R_r is the secondary resistance per phase, L_{sr} is the magnetizing inductance per phase, L_s is the primary inductance per phase, L_r is the secondary inductance per phase, F_L is the load disturbance, D_m is the viscous friction and iron-loss coefficient, n_p is the number of pole pairs, and T is the sample period [26].

3.3.3.2 Neural Observer Design

The RHONO proposed to estimate (3.42) is designed as follows:

$$\hat{x}_1(k+1) = w_{11}S(\hat{x}_1(k)) + w_{12}\hat{x}_2(k) + g_1e(k),$$

$$\hat{x}_2(k+1) = w_{21}S(\hat{x}_2(k)) + w_{22}S(\hat{x}_3(k)) + w_{23}S(\hat{x}_4(k)) + w_{24}S(\hat{x}_2(k))S(\hat{x}_4(k))$$
$$+ w_{25}S(\hat{x}_3(k))S(\hat{x}_4(k)) + w_{26}S(\hat{x}_2(k))S(\hat{x}_3(k))$$
$$- w_vS(\hat{x}_3(k))\sin(n_p\hat{x}_1(k)) + S(\hat{x}_4(k))\cos(n_p\hat{x}_1(k)))\hat{x}_5(k)$$
$$+ w_vS(\hat{x}_3(k))\cos(n_p\hat{x}_1(k)) - S(\hat{x}_4(k))\sin(n_p\hat{x}_1(k)))\hat{x}_6(k) + g_2e(k),$$

$$\hat{x}_3(k+1) = w_{31}S(\hat{x}_2(k)) + w_{32}S(\hat{x}_3(k)) + w_{33}S(\hat{x}_2(k))S(\hat{x}_3(k))$$
$$+ w_{34}S(\hat{x}_1(k))S(\hat{x}_2(k)) + w_{35}S(\hat{x}_1(k))S(\hat{x}_3(k))$$
$$+ w_{fa}\cos(n_p\hat{x}_1(k))\hat{x}_5(k) + w_{fa}\sin(n_p\hat{x}_1(k))\hat{x}_6 + g_3e(k),$$

$$\hat{x}_4(k+1) = w_{41}S(\hat{x}_2(k)) + w_{42}S(\hat{x}_4(k)) + w_{43}S(\hat{x}_2(k))S(\hat{x}_4(k))$$
$$+ w_{44}S(\hat{x}_1(k))S(\hat{x}_2(k)) + w_{45}S(\hat{x}_1(k))S(\hat{x}_4(k))$$
$$- w_{fa}\sin(n_p\hat{x}_1(k))\hat{x}_5(k) + w_{fa}\cos(n_p\hat{x}_1(k))\hat{x}_6 + g_4e(k),$$

$$\hat{x}_5(k+1) = w_{51}S(\hat{x}_2(k)) + w_{52}S(\hat{x}_3(k)) + w_{53}S(\hat{x}_4(k))$$
$$+ w_{54}S(\hat{x}_5(k)) + w_{55}S(\hat{x}_2(k))S(\hat{x}_3(k)) + w_{56}S(\hat{x}_2(k))S(\hat{x}_4(k))$$
$$+ w_{57}S(\hat{x}_3(k))S(\hat{x}_4(k)) + w_{58}u_\alpha(k) + g_5e(k),$$

$$\hat{x}_6(k+1) = w_{61}S(\hat{x}_2(k)) + w_{62}S(\hat{x}_3(k)) + w_{63}S(\hat{x}_4(k))$$
$$+ w_{64}S(\hat{x}_6(k)) + w_{65}S(\hat{x}_2(k))S(\hat{x}_3(k)) + w_{66}S(\hat{x}_2(k))S(\hat{x}_4(k))$$
$$+ w_{67}S(\hat{x}_3(k))S(\hat{x}_4(k)) + w_{68}u_\beta(k) + g_6e(k), \tag{3.43}$$

where $S(x(k)) = \alpha\tan h(\beta x(k)) + \gamma$, $\hat{x}_1(k)$ is used to estimate $q_m(k)$, $\hat{x}_2(k)$ to estimate $v(k)$, $\hat{x}_3(k)$ to estimate $\psi_\alpha(k)$, $\hat{x}_4(k)$ to estimate $\psi_\beta(k)$, $\hat{x}_5(k)$ to estimate $i_\alpha(k)$, and $\hat{x}_6(k)$ to estimate $i_\beta(k)$. Both the NN and LIM states are initialized at random. The associated covariance matrices are initialized as diagonals, and the nonzero elements are: $P_i(0) = 100{,}000$; $Q_i(0) = 1000$, and $R_i(0) = 10{,}000$ ($i = 1, \ldots, 6$), respectively. The input signals u_α and u_β are selected as chirp functions. The simulation results are presented in Figs. 3.24–3.31. They display the time evolution of the estimated states and the disturbances and uncertainties applied, respectively. It is important to note that the above neural model can be used for controller synthesis, without previous knowledge of the plant model or of its parameters. Hence, Eq. (3.42) only serves as a guide to design the neural observer (3.43).

3.3.3.3 Real-Time Results

For the real-time implementation, the neural observer designed in Section 3.3.2.1 was used to observe an actual LIM. It was designed to estimate both the α–β model of the LIM and its state variable signals with linear output. The steps for real-time implementation are:

1. A Simulink® model representing the control scheme is loaded into the controller board dSPACE® DS1104 using the dSPACE® software, the RTI1104 libraries, and ControlDesk®. The LIM model used was an LAB

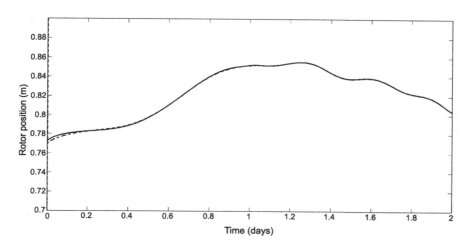

FIGURE 3.24 Time evolution for rotor position (solid line) and its estimate $\widehat{x}_1(k)$ (dashed line).

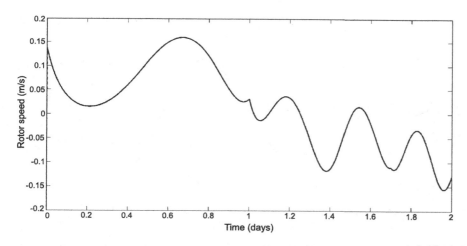

FIGURE 3.25 Time evolution for rotor speed (solid line) and its estimate $\widehat{x}_2(k)$ (dashed line).

– Volt® 8228. The inputs to the LIM were a frequency-varying signal given by an autotransformer and a PWM control coupled signal through a dSPACE® DS1104 Board and RTI 1104 Connector Panel. Both signals were sent through a power module which allows managing required voltages and currents to move the secondary of the LIM.

2. The α-axis and β-axis currents were obtained from the three actual LIM currents which were converted using the α–β model [26]. Position and velocity were obtained from the precision linear encoder SENC® 150 (SENC is a registered trademark of ACU-RITE) mounted on the LIM.

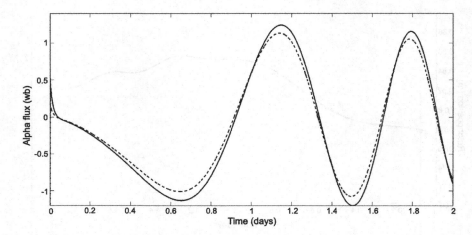

FIGURE 3.26 Time evolution for alpha flux (solid line) and its estimate $\widehat{x}_3\,(k)$ (dashed line).

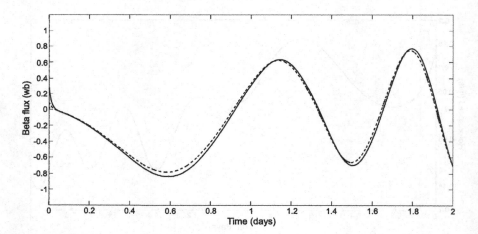

FIGURE 3.27 Time evolution for beta flux (solid line) and its estimate $\widehat{x}_4\,(k)$ (dashed line).

3. The fixed weights values of the observer were: $\omega_{14} = 0.001$, $\omega_{15} = 0.001$, $\omega_f = 0.001$, $\omega_{45} = 0.02178$, and $\omega_{55} = 0.02178$. We also assumed $np = 4$, $k_4 = 0.0964$, and $k_6 = 124.08$.
4. The values for the Kalman filter were initialized randomly.
5. Position, velocity, currents, and fluxes became the estimated signals. The neural observer used the EKF based training algorithm (3.8) in order to adjust its weights $w_{ij}(k)$ at each sampling time k.

It is important to remark that the EKF used to develop the RHONN was an online learning algorithm, and it was performed using a parallel configuration

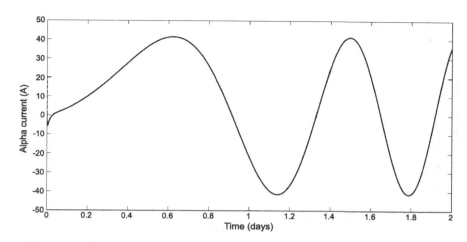

FIGURE 3.28 Time evolution for alpha current (solid line) and its estimate $\widehat{x}_5(k)$ (dashed line).

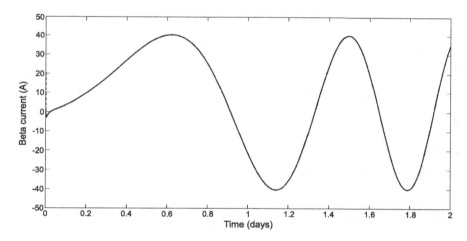

FIGURE 3.29 Time evolution for beta current (solid line) and its estimate $\widehat{x}_6(k)$ (dashed line).

between samplings. All the neural states and the weight vectors were initialized randomly, without any restriction on their initialization. It is important to remark that the initial conditions of the plant were completely different from the initial conditions for the neural observer.

The experiments were performed with an observer scheme as depicted in Fig. 3.32 and the benchmark shown in Fig. 3.33.

The results of the real-time implementation are presented as follows: Fig. 3.34 displays the estimation performance for the position; Fig. 3.35 presents the velocity performance, Figs. 3.36 and 3.37 present the estimation performance

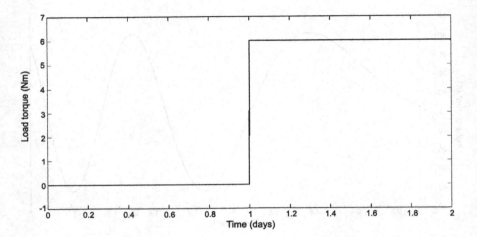

FIGURE 3.30 Applied load.

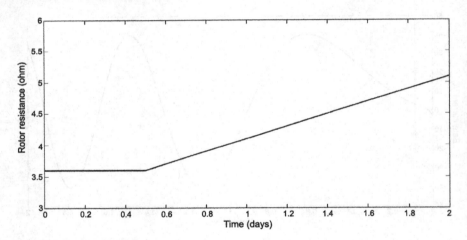

FIGURE 3.31 Rotor resistance.

for the fluxes in phase α and β, respectively. Figs. 3.38 and 3.39 portray the estimation performance for currents in phase α and β, respectively.

It is important to note that the real-time flux signal is not available; however, in order to establish a comparison, the RHONO signals were compared to those computed from a nonlinear observer, as in Section 3.3.2.2.

3.3.4 Anaerobic Digestion

Anaerobic digestion is a biological complex process which develops in the absence of oxygen [28]. It is commonly used to treat wastewater with high

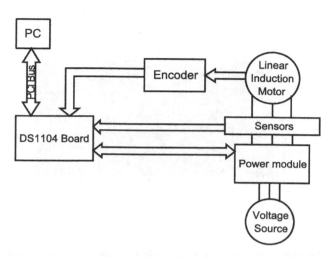

FIGURE 3.32 Schematic representation of the control prototype.

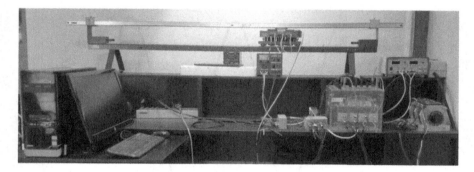

FIGURE 3.33 Benchmark for linear induction motor.

organic load: the pollutants (substrate) are degraded by means of anaerobic microorganisms (biomass), producing a biogas mainly composed of methane (CH_4) and carbon dioxide (CO_2).

Anaerobic digestion is very sensitive to operating conditions. Additionally, some variables are difficult to measure due to technical or economical constraints, i.e., the substrate consumption measurement is expensive, needs three hours, and is done off-line [29]. Biomass measurement is even more restrictive because the existing sensors are designed using a biological approach, and are not adequate for automatic control. For this reason, the first step required for control analysis and design is to develop state observers in order to estimate unmeasured variables [30].

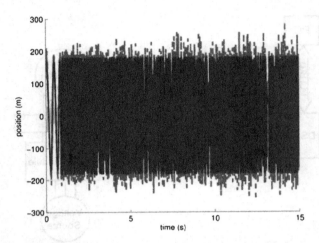

FIGURE 3.34 Position estimation, plant signal (solid line), neural observer (dashed line) and estimation error (pointed–dashed line).

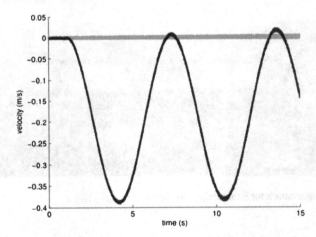

FIGURE 3.35 Velocity estimation, plant signal (solid line), neural observer (dashed line) and estimation error (pointed–dashed line).

3.3.4.1 Process Description

Organic waste is degraded in four successive stages (the products of one stage are the input for the next): hidrolysis, aciodogenesis, acetogenesis, and methanogenesis (Fig. 3.40). Each stage is run by a different bacteria population and therefore presents different biological, physic chemical, and hydrodynamic phenomena [37].

The speed of each stage development is also different; the acidogenesis and acetogenesis are very fast stages; hydrolysis is fast, and finally, methanogene-

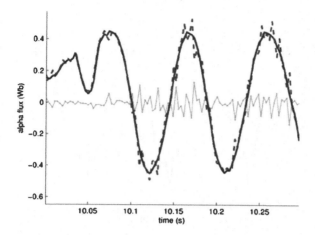

FIGURE 3.36 Alpha flux estimation, plant signal (solid line), neural observer (dashed line) and estimation error (pointed–dashed line).

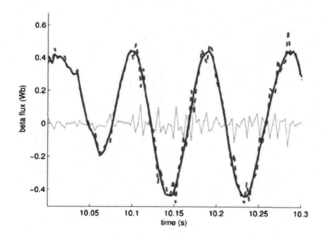

FIGURE 3.37 Beta flux estimation, plant signal (solid line), neural observer (dashed line) and estimation error (pointed–dashed line).

sis is the slowest and the most important for the process stability. In general, anaerobic digestion is very sensitive to variations in the operating conditions such as pH, temperature, overload on substrate concentration, etc. [36].

In this case, a completely stirred tank reactor is considered (Fig. 3.41). This kind of reactor is currently used in industrial processes because its hydrodynamic behavior is relatively easy to model and control. The substrate S_1, S_2 is fed to the reactor with a flow rate Q_{in} (dilution rate $D_{in} = Q_{in}/V$ where V is the reactor volume), IC and Z are fed at same flow. Inside the reactor, the substrate

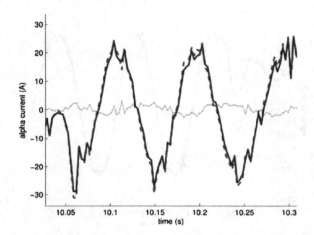

FIGURE 3.38 Alpha current estimation, plant signal (solid line), neural observer (dashed line) and estimation error (pointed–dashed line).

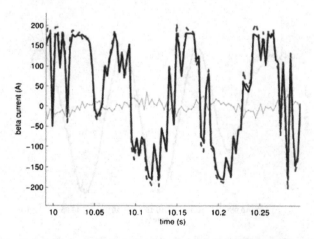

FIGURE 3.39 Beta current estimation, plant signal (solid line), neural observer (dashed line) and estimation error (pointed–dashed line).

is treated by the biomass, and then residual substrate (pollution) is removed at the same flow rate, $Q_{in} = Q_{out}$. The biomass filter is used to improve the substrate treatment: bacteria cannot go out of the reactor; hence, one avoids the washout and enhances performance. In practice, the biomass is fixed in a solid support to get the biomass filter behavior. The model considers this condition in the biomass equations, where k_{d1}, k_{d2} denote the death rates, which represent the biomass falling down from the support and becoming inactive [36–38].

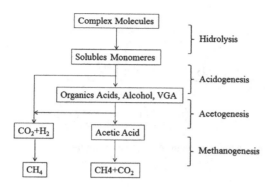

FIGURE 3.40 Anaerobic digestion stages.

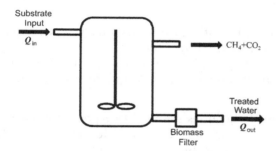

FIGURE 3.41 Completely stirred tank reactor with biomass filter.

3.3.4.2 Process Model

For modeling purposes, the organic components of the substrate considered in this example are classified as *equivalent glucose* (S_1) and *equivalent acetate* (S_2). The first one is assumed to model complex molecules, and the second one represents molecules which are transformed directly into acetic acid. Biomass is also classified into two types, denoted X_1 and X_2. X_1 represent the population of bacteria which transform *equivalent glucose* substrates. X_2 stands for bacteria degrading *equivalent acetate* substrates. This classification allows the process to be represented by only two stages: the methanogenesis, which is the limiting one (the most interesting for automatic control and energy approaches), and a preliminary stage. Such a representation of anaerobic digestion is depicted in the functional scheme of Fig. 3.42 [36,39].

The physico-chemical phenomena (acid–base equilibrium and mass conservation) are modeled by five algebraic equations:

$$HS + S^- - S_2 = 0, \tag{3.44}$$
$$H^+ S^- - K_a HS = 0,$$
$$H^+ B - K_b CO_{2d} = 0,$$

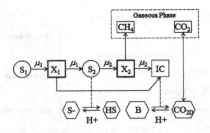

FIGURE 3.42 Functional scheme of anaerobic digestion process.

$$B + CO_{2d} - IC = 0,$$
$$B + S^- - Z = 0,$$

where IC is the inorganic carbon, HS is non-ionized acetic acid (mol L^{-1}), S^- ionized acetic acid (mol L^{-1}), H^+ ionized hydrogen (mol L^{-1}), B measures bicarbonate (mol L^{-1}), CO_{2d} is dissolved carbon dioxide (mol L^{-1}), K_a is an acid–base equilibrium constant, K_b is an equilibrium constant between B and CO_{2d}.

Ordinary differential equations are used to represent biomass growth, substrate transformations, inorganic carbon evolution (result of the biological phase), and cations which are biologically inert:

$$\frac{dX_1}{dt} = (\mu_1 - k_{d1})X_1, \tag{3.45}$$
$$\frac{dS_1}{dt} = -R_6\mu_1 X_1 + D_{in}(S_{1in} - S_1),$$
$$\frac{dX_2}{dt} = (\mu_2 - k_{d2})X_2,$$
$$\frac{dS_2}{dt} = -R_3\mu_2 X_2 + R_4\mu_1 X_1 + D_{in}(S_{1in} - S_1),$$
$$\frac{dIC}{dt} = R_2 R_3\mu_2 X_2 + R_5\mu_1 X_1 - \lambda R_1 R_3\mu_2 X_2 + D_{in}(IC_{in} - IC),$$
$$\frac{dZ}{dt} = D_{in}(Z_{in} - Z),$$

where μ_1 is the growth rate (Haldane type) of X_1 (h^{-1}), μ_2 the growth rate (Haldane type) of X_2 (h^{-1}), k_{d1} the death rate of X_1 (mol L^{-1}), k_{d2} the death rate of X_2 (mol L^{-1}), D_{in} the dilution rate (h^{-1}), S_{1in} the fast degradable substrate input (mol L^{-1}), S_{2in} the slow degradable substrate input (mol L^{-1}), IC inorganic carbon (mol L^{-1}), Z the total of cations (mol L^{-1}), IC_{in} the inorganic carbon input (mol L^{-1}), λ is a coefficient considered in the law of partial pressure for the dissolved CO_2, and R_1, R_2, R_3, R_4, R_5, and R_6 are the yield coefficients.

Finally, the gaseous phase considered in the process output is represented by:

$$Y_{CH_4} = R_1 R_2 \mu_2 X_2, \tag{3.46}$$
$$Y_{CO_2} = \lambda R_3 R_2 \mu_2 X_2,$$

with

$$\lambda = \frac{CO_{2D}}{P_t K_h - CO_{2D}} \tag{3.47}$$

where P_t is the atmospheric pressure and K_h is the Henry constant; moreover,

$$CO_{2D} = \frac{H^+ IC}{K_b + H^+}, \tag{3.48}$$

$$H^+ = 10^{-pH}. \tag{3.49}$$

This model will be used in order to validate the observer structure and is considered unknown.

3.3.4.3 Neural State Observer

A common problem of bioprocesses is the variables' measurement [36–41]. For anaerobic digestion there are two special variables which present restrictions for measurement. Substrate is directly related to Chemical Oxygen Demand, which is determined off-line by chemical analysis requiring at least two hours. On the other hand, the existing biomass sensors are expensive and are designed from a biological viewpoint. These situations are not convenient for designing efficient control strategies. In order to solve these problems, it is important to develop state observers which allow estimating the hard to measure variables.

Several observers have been proposed in order to estimate such variables, namely linear observers, asymptotic observer based on nonlinear model, closed loop observer, interval observer, fuzzy observer, among others [36–41]. Each approach presents advantages and inconveniences, such as difficulties to design, tune and implement, as well as numerical instability due to ill-conditioning of the process dynamics, estimation errors due to model uncertainties, etc.

In this section, the RHONO with nonlinear output presented in Section 3.2 is applied for anaerobic digestion process. The objective is to mainly estimate the biomass and substrate, which are good indicators of the biological activity inside the reactors and important for supervision and control purposes. The neural observer is based on the approximation from output measurements; for anaerobic digestion methane and carbon dioxide are measured.

As said before, anaerobic digestion has fast and slow dynamics. Usually, the main interest is focused on slow dynamics since it imposes the global dynamics of the process; additionally, the slow stage is the most sensitive to variations of the operating conditions. The associated state variables with slow stages are S_2 and X_2. IC is a product of the substrate degradation and, even if it can be measured, it is advisable to estimate IC. Cations are also present in the slow stage but they are biologically inert. The observer designed in this section is devoted to estimating the biomass X_2 and substrate S_2. Fig. 3.4 shows a schematic diagram of the neural observer.

3.3.4.4 RHONO for Biomass X_2 Estimation

The objective of this RHONO for biomass X_2 is to estimate bacteria which degrade substrate *equivalent acetate*. A parallel representation is considered for the RHONO and an online weights adaptation; additionally, it is supposed for this case that there are available measurements for S_2, IC, and pH [36].

The observer structure is given by next equation:

$$\hat{X}_2(k+1) = w_1(k)S^{10}(\hat{X}_2(k))S^{12}(S_2(k))S^2(IC(k)) \tag{3.50}$$
$$+ w_2(k)(k)S^2(\hat{X}_2(k))S^4(S_2(k))S^2(IC(k))$$
$$+ w_3(k)(k)S^{15}(\hat{X}_2(k))S^8(S_2(k))S^2(IC(k))$$
$$+ w_4(k)(k)S^{15}(\hat{X}_2(k))S^{15}(S_2(k))S^2(IC(k))$$
$$+ w_5(k)S^{15}(\hat{X}_2(k)) + w_6(k)S^{15}(\hat{X}_2(k))S^7(S_2(k))S^2(IC(k))$$
$$+ w_7(k)S^{15}(\hat{X}_2(k))S^2(IC(k))$$
$$+ w_8(k)S^{15}(\hat{X}_2(k))S^{15}(S_2(k))S^2(IC(k)) + Le(k)$$

where $L \in \Re^{1 \times 2}$ is selected empirically as $L = \begin{bmatrix} 0.19 & 0.1 \end{bmatrix}$. The NN outputs are represented by

$$\hat{Y}_{CH_4} = R_1 R_2 \mu_2 \hat{X}_2, \tag{3.51}$$
$$\hat{Y}_{CO_2} = \lambda R_2 R_3 \mu_2 \hat{X}_2,$$

with λ as in (3.47).

Initialization is done as follows: the NN state X_2 is initialized randomly; covariance matrix is a unit matrix, $H(0) = 0$ since the NN outputs do not depend directly on the weight vector as described in (2.15). In order to verify the observer performance, a disturbance is injected on the input substrate as shown in Fig. 3.43. The square signal amplitude is 30% of the input substrate. It is supposed that the disturbance is not measured and hence it is assumed as an external disturbance. The disturbance is incepted at $t = 120$ h in order to assure an equilibrium point in the process, and it is eliminated at $t = 650$ h to guarantee that the bacteria have reached the steady state. The obtained result from simulations is shown in Fig. 3.44.

An exact estimation of biomass is done by the neural observer; moreover, there is no transience when the disturbance is incepted and eliminated. This behavior proves that the NN has learnt the complex dynamics of the process fast. On

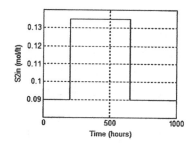

FIGURE 3.43 Input substrate S_{2in}.

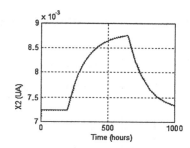

FIGURE 3.44 Time evolution of the biomass X_2 (solid line) and its estimate $\hat{X}_2$ (dashed line).

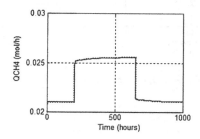

FIGURE 3.45 CH_4 model output (solid line) and neural network output (dashed line).

the other hand, the observer outputs are compared with those of the process. The result of this comparison is shown in Figs. 3.45 and 3.46.

Different operating conditions are considered in order to verify the observer robustness. Disturbances on input inorganic carbon and dilution rate are intercepted simultaneously at $t = 300$ h and eliminated at $t = 750$ h, as shown in Fig. 3.47. The amplitude of these disturbances is 20% of the initial values for both variables. These inputs are measured variables, which can be manipulated for control purposes. They are not included in the observer structure in order to illustrate the robustness and the properties of the NN to approximate

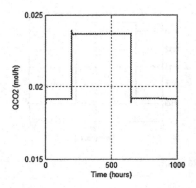

FIGURE 3.46 CO_2 model output (solid line) and neural network output (dashed line).

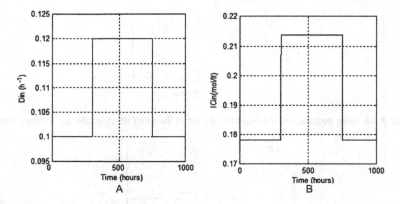

A

B

FIGURE 3.47 (A) Dilution rate D_{in}, (B) Inorganic carbon input IC_{in}.

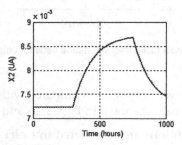

FIGURE 3.48 Time evolution of the biomass X_2 (solid line) and its estimate (dashed line).

complex nonlinear functions. Fig. 3.48 shows the obtained results considering these operating conditions.

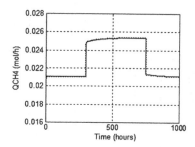

FIGURE 3.49 CH_4 model output (solid line) and neural network output (dashed line).

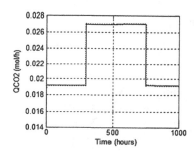

FIGURE 3.50 CO_2 model output (solid line) and neural network output (dashed line).

The neural observer converges fast to the process behavior. The considered disturbances do not affect the variables' estimation. Figs. 3.49 and 3.50 show the output comparison.

3.3.4.5 RHONO for Substrate S_2 Estimation

An RHONO for equivalent acetate substrate estimation is designed supposing that measurements for X_2 and pH are available [36]. The observer structure is presented below:

$$\hat{S}_2(k+1) = w_1(k)S(\hat{S}_2(k)) + w_2(k)S^3(\hat{S}_2(k))D_{in}(k) \qquad (3.52)$$
$$+ w_4(k)D_{in}(k) + Le(k)$$

where $L \in \Re^{1 \times 2}$ is selected empirically as $L = \begin{bmatrix} 0.01 & 0.01 \end{bmatrix}$. The NN outputs are:

$$\hat{Y}_{CH_4} = R_1 R_2 \hat{\mu}_2 X_2, \qquad (3.53)$$
$$\hat{Y}_{CO_2} = \lambda R_2 R_3 \hat{\mu}_2 X_2,$$

where λ is computed using (3.47). For initialization, the NN state is initialized with random values, the covariance matrix is set to be a unit matrix, $H(0) = 0$.

In order to verify the observer performance, a disturbance is injected on the input substrate as shown in Fig. 3.51. This square signal amplitude is 30% of the input substrate. It is supposed that this disturbance is not measured and

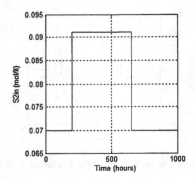

FIGURE 3.51 Substrate input S_{2in}.

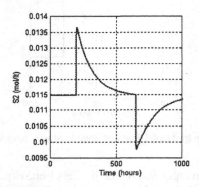

FIGURE 3.52 Time evolution of the substrate S_2 (solid line) and its estimate $\hat{S}_2$ (dashed line).

thus it is assumed as an external one. The disturbance is incepted at $t = 200$ h in order to assure an equilibrium point in the process, and it is eliminated at $t = 650$ h to guarantee that bacteria have reached the steady state. The obtained result from simulations is shown in Fig. 3.52.

An exact estimation of substrate is done by the neural observer; moreover, there is no transience when the disturbance is incepted and eliminated. Once again, this behavior proves that the NN has learnt the complex dynamics of the process fast. On the other hand, the observer outputs are compared with those of the process. The results of this comparison are shown in Figs. 3.53 and 3.54.

3.3.4.6   RHONO for Inorganic Carbon IC Estimation

The same representation as for X_2 and S_2 estimation is considered in this case, too [36]. It is supposed that measurements for X_2, S_2, and pH are available. The observer structure is shown below:

$$I\hat{C}(k+1) = w_1(k)S(I\hat{C}(k)) + w_2(k)S(I\hat{C}(k))S^3(S_2(k))S^2(X_2(k)) \tag{3.54}$$
$$+ w_3(k)S(I\hat{C}(k))S(S_2(k))S(X_2(k)) + w_4(k)S^2(I\hat{C}(k)) + Le(k)$$

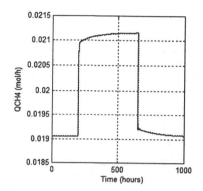

FIGURE 3.53 CH_4 model output (solid line) and neural network output (dashed line).

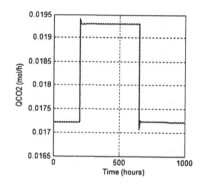

FIGURE 3.54 CO_2 model output (solid line) and neural network output (dashed line).

where $L \in \Re^{1 \times 2}$ is selected empirically as $L = \begin{bmatrix} 1 \times 10^{-7} & 1 \times 10^{-4} \end{bmatrix}$. The NN outputs are given by:

$$\hat{Y}_{CH_4} = R_1 R_2 \mu_2 X_2, \tag{3.55}$$
$$\hat{Y}_{CO_2} = \hat{\lambda} R_2 R_3 \mu_2 X_2$$

where $\hat{\lambda}$ has the same form as in (3.47), but it is computed in this case taking into account the estimated $\hat{IC}$ supplied by the RHONO.

For the initialization, the NN state IC is initialized with a random value near the initial condition of the process variable, the covariance matrix is set as a diagonal matrix $P(0) = 1.0051 \times 10^4$ and $Q(0) = 0.705$; finally, $H(0) = 0$.

In order to verify the observer performance, a disturbance is incepted on the input substrate as shown in Fig. 3.55. This square signal amplitude is 30% of the input substrate. It is supposed that this disturbance is not measured and thus it is assumed as an external disturbance. The disturbance is incepted at $t = 200$ h in order to assure an equilibrium point in the process, and it is

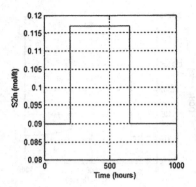

FIGURE 3.55 Substrate input S_{2in}.

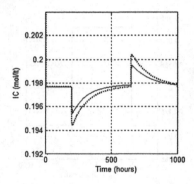

FIGURE 3.56 Time evolution inorganic carbon IC (solid line) and its estimate $\hat{IC}$ (dashed line).

eliminated at $t = 650$ h to guarantee that the bacteria have reached the steady state. The obtained result from simulations is shown in Fig. 3.56.

As for previous cases, the observer outputs are compared with those of the process. The result of this comparison is shown in Figs. 3.57 and 3.58.

The estimated variable converges to the real one; however, when a disturbance on the input substrate is considered, a transient error is present, which is eliminated when $t \to \infty$. The possible reason for this performance is that the inorganic carbon observer structure does not include the dynamics of biomass X_1.

3.3.4.7 RHONO for Biomass X_2 and Substrate S_2 Estimation

The last application of RHONO in this section is the simultaneous estimation of X_2 and S_2 [36]. In this case, we supposed that measurements for IC and pH are available. The observer structure is

$$\hat{X}_2(k+1) = w_{11}(k)S^3(\hat{S}_2(k)) + w_{21}(k)S(\hat{S}_2(k))S(\hat{X}_2(k)) \tag{3.56}$$

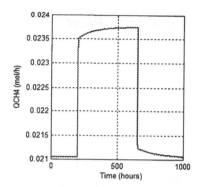

FIGURE 3.57 CH_4 model output (solid line) and neural network output (dashed line).

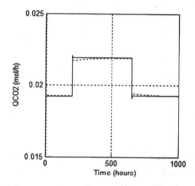

FIGURE 3.58 CO_2 model output (solid line) and neural network output (dashed line).

$$+ w_{31}(k)S(\hat{X}_2(k)) + w_{41}(k)S(\hat{X}_2(k)S(\hat{S}_2(k))D_e$$
$$+ w_{51}(k)S(D_e) + w_{61}(k)S(\hat{S}_2(k))S^5(\hat{X}_2(k)) + L_1 e(k),$$
$$\hat{S}_2(k+1) = w_{12}(k)S^3(\hat{X}_2(k)) + w_{22}(k)S^2(\hat{X}_2(k))S^2(\hat{S}_2(k))$$
$$+ w_{32}(k)S^2(\hat{X}_2(k)) + w_{42}(k)S^3(\hat{X}_2(k)S^5(\hat{S}_2(k))D_e$$
$$+ w_{52}(k)S^6(\hat{X}_2(k))S^3(\hat{S}_2(k))$$
$$+ w_{62}(k)S^2(\hat{S}_2(k)) + L_2 e(k),$$

where $L_1, L_2 \in \Re^{1 \times 2}$ are selected empirically as

$$L_1 = \begin{bmatrix} 1 \times 10^2 & 1 \times 10^3 \end{bmatrix},$$
$$L_2 = \begin{bmatrix} 1 \times 10^7 & 1 \end{bmatrix}.$$

The NN outputs are

$$\hat{Y}_{CH_4} = R_1 R_2 \hat{\mu}_2 \hat{X}_2, \tag{3.57}$$
$$\hat{Y}_{CO_2} = \lambda R_2 R_3 \hat{\mu}_2 \hat{X}_2$$

Table 3.2 Covariance matrices EFK for RHONO

$P_i(0)$	$Q_i(0)$	$R_i(0)$	
$(1 \times 10^{10})\, I_{9 \times 9}$	$(1.3 \times 10^{-2})\, I_{9 \times 9}$	$R_1(0) = \begin{bmatrix} 70 & 0 \\ 0 & 1500 \end{bmatrix}$	
$(7.9 \times 10^{4})\, I_{6 \times 6}$	$(1 \times 10^{-7})\, I_{6 \times 6}$	$R_2(0) = \begin{bmatrix} 850 & 0 \\ 0 & 80 \end{bmatrix}$	

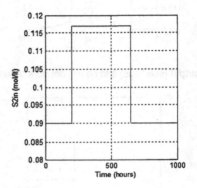

FIGURE 3.59 Substrate input S_{2in}.

where λ is computed using (3.47). For the initialization, the NN states X_2 and S_2 are initialized with random values near the initial condition of the process variables, the covariance matrices are set as diagonal matrices (see Table 3.2); finally, $H(0) = 0$.

In order to study the observer behavior, a disturbance is incepted on the input substrate as shown in Fig. 3.59. This square signal amplitude is 30% of the input substrate. It is supposed that the disturbance is not measured and thus it is assumed as an external one. The disturbance is incepted at $t = 200$ h in order to assure an equilibrium point in the process, and it is stopped at $t = 650$ h to guarantee that the bacteria have reached the steady state. The obtained results from simulations are shown in Figs. 3.60 and 3.61.

The observer convergence is clear at the beginning of simulations. However, when a disturbance is injected, a small transient error is present in the biomass estimation, this error is eliminated in a few hours. However, when the disturbance is eliminated, a larger error is induced, and it does not totally vanish with $t \to \infty$. The error is present also for the substrate estimation and it is larger than the one for biomass estimation. Nevertheless, it is important to remark that the qualitative estimation of the two variables is done well by the neural observer, which means that the observer does not lose its properties when approximating the complex dynamics of anaerobic digestion, even in the presence of changes on the operating conditions. As for the inorganic

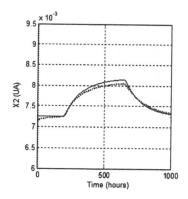

FIGURE 3.60 Time evolution of the biomass X_2 (solid line) and its estimate $\hat{X}_2$ (dashed line).

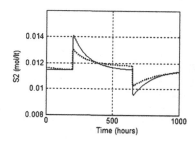

FIGURE 3.61 Time evolution of the substrate S_2 (solid line) and its estimate $\hat{S}_2$ (dashed line).

carbon observer case, this performance is such because in the real process the dynamics of the substrate is influenced by other variables, and not included in the model structure. Thus, to improve the observer performance it is required to include them.

Figs. 3.62 and 3.63 present a comparison between estimated outputs and process outputs. A similar behavior as for biomass and substrate estimation is obtained.

Different operating conditions are considered in order to verify the observer robustness. Disturbances on input inorganic carbon and dilution rate are incepted simultaneously at $t = 300$ h and eliminated at $t = 750$ h as shown in Fig. 3.64. The disturbance amplitude is 10% of the initial values of both variables. Inorganic carbon is not included in the observer structure; thus, the disturbance on IC_{in} is considered as an external one. Figs. 3.65 and 3.66 show the obtained results considering these operating conditions.

As for previous cases, the observer convergence is present at the beginning of simulations. When a disturbance is incepted (and eliminated), a small tran-

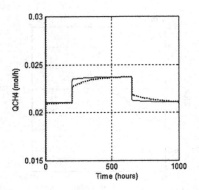

FIGURE 3.62 CH_4 model output (solid line) and neural network output (dashed line).

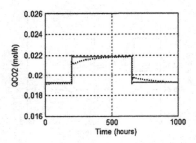

FIGURE 3.63 CO_2 model output (solid line) and neural network output (dashed line).

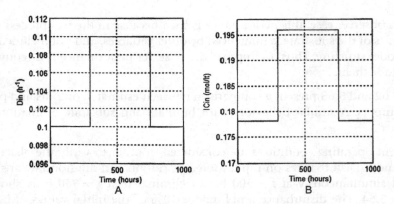

FIGURE 3.64 (A) Dilution rate D_{in}, (B) Inorganic carbon input IC_{in}.

sient error is observable in the biomass and substrate estimation. This error vanishes as $t \rightarrow \infty$.

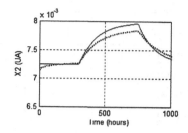

FIGURE 3.65 Time evolution of the biomass X_2 (solid line) and its estimate $\hat{X}_2$ (dashed line).

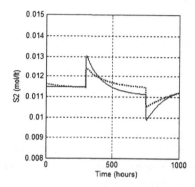

FIGURE 3.66 Time evolution of the substrate S_2 (solid line) and its estimate $\hat{S}_2$ (dashed line).

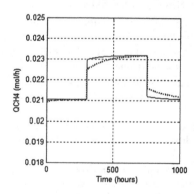

FIGURE 3.67 CH_4 model output (solid line) and neural network output (dashed line).

Figs. 3.67 and 3.68 present a comparison between estimated outputs and process outputs. A similar behavior as for biomass and substrate estimation is obtained.

In general, it can be remarked that for all the considered operating conditions the observer is able to approximate the process behavior even if a small error is

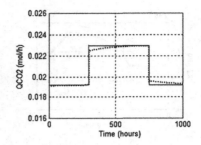

FIGURE 3.68 CO_2 model output (solid line) and neural network output (dashed line).

present. When the disturbance is incepted, there is neither oscillation nor over-shoot. This is an important advantage for control purposes since the estimated variables should be included in control strategies.

REFERENCES

[1] A.Y. Alanis, E.N. Sanchez, A.G. Loukianov, M.A. Perez, Real-time recurrent neural state estimation, IEEE Transactions on Neural Networks 22 (3) (Mar. 2011) 497–505.

[2] S. Haykin, Kalman Filtering and Neural Networks, John Wiley and Sons, NY, USA, 2001.

[3] H. Khalil, Nonlinear Systems, 2nd ed., Prentice Hall, Upper Saddle River, NJ, USA, 1996.

[4] G.A. Rovithakis, M.A. Chistodoulou, Adaptive Control with Recurrent High-Order Neural Networks, Springer-Verlag, New York, USA, 2000.

[5] V. Utkin, J. Guldner, J. Shi, Sliding Mode Control in Electromechanical Systems, Taylor and Francis, Philadelphia, USA, 1999.

[6] A.G. Loukianov, J. Rivera, J.M. Cañedo, Discrete time sliding mode control of an induction motor, in: Proceedings IFAC'02, Barcelona, Spain, July 2002.

[7] Z. Andonov, Overview of induction motor parameter identification techniques, in: Proceedings of the 11th International Symposium on Power Electronics, Novi Sad, Yugoslavia, Nov. 2001.

[8] M. Elbuluk, L. Tong, I. Husain, Neural-network-based model reference adaptive systems for high-performance motor drives and motion controls, IEEE Transactions on Industry Applications 38 (3) (May 2002).

[9] J. Liang, Z. Wang, X. Liu, State estimation for coupled uncertain stochastic networks with missing measurements and time-varying delays: the discrete-time case, IEEE Transactions on Neural Networks 20 (5) (May 2009) 781–793.

[10] W. Leonard, Control of Electrical Drives, 2nd ed., Springer-Verlag, 2001.

[11] F. Khorrami, P. Krishnamurthy, H. Melkote, Modeling and Adaptive Nonlinear Control of Electric Motors, Springer-Verlag, Berlin, Germany, 2003.

[12] F. Chen, M.W. Dunnigan, Comparative study of a sliding-mode observer and Kalman filters for full state estimation in an induction machine, IEE Proceedings – Electric Power Applications 149 (2008) 53–64.

[13] D.F. Coutinho, L.P.F.A. Pereira, A robust Luenberger-like observer for induction machines, in: Proceedings IEEE IECON 2005, Nov. 2005.

[14] J. Li, Y. Zhong, Comparison of three Kalman filters for speed estimation of induction machines, in: Proceedings Industry Applications Conference 2005, Oct. 2005.

[15] H.K. Khalil, E.G. Strangas, S. Jurkovic, Speed Observer and Reduced Nonlinear Model for Sensorless Control of Induction Motors, IEEE Transactions on Control Systems Technology 17 (2) (Mar. 2009) 327–339.

[16] L. Gang, Artificial immune controller for PMSM speed regulation system, in: IEEE Fifth International Conference on Bio-Inspired Computing: Theories and Applications (BIC-TA), 2010, p. 582.

[17] H.T. Yazdi, C. Grantham, On line rotor parameter determination of three phase induction motors, in: Proceedings of the International Conference on Power Electronics and Drive Systems, 1995, pp. 819–824.

[18] L. Ljung, System Identification: Theory for the User, 2nd ed., Prentice Hall, Upper Saddle River, NJ, USA, 1999.

[19] M. Norgaard, O. Ravn, N.K. Poulsen, L.K. Hansen, Neural Networks for Modelling and Control of Dynamic Systems, Springer-Verlag, New York, USA, 2000.

[20] T. Söderström, P. Stoica, System Identification, Prentice Hall, London, UK, 1989.

[21] J.F. Gieras, Linear Inductions Drives, Oxford University Press, Oxford, England, 1994.

[22] I. Boldea, S.A. Nasar, Linear Electric Actuators and Generators, Cambridge University Press, Cambridge, England, 1997.

[23] I. Takahashi, Y. Ide, Decoupling control of thrust and attractive force of a LIM using a space vector control inverter, IEEE Transactions on Industry Applications 29 (Jan./Feb. 1993) 161–167.

[24] E.R. Laithwaite, F.T. Barwell, Linear induction motors for high-speed railways, Electronics and Power 10 (4) (Apr. 1964) 100–103.

[25] G.K. Venayagamoorthy, Smart grid and electric transportation, in: 12th International IEEE Conference on Intelligent Transportation Systems, St. Louis, MO, USA, Oct. 2009, pp. 1–2.

[26] V.H. Benitez, Block Neural Control: Application to a Linear Induction Motor, in Spanish, Master's Thesis, Cinvestav, Unidad Guadalajara, Mexico, 2002.

[27] N. Kazantzis, C. Kravaris, Time-discretization of nonlinear control systems via Taylor methods, Computers & Chemical Engineering 23 (1999) 763–784.

[28] S. Carlos-Hernandez, J.F. Beteau, E.N. Sanchez, Design and real-time implementation of a TS fuzzy observer for anaerobic wastewater treatment plants, in: IEEE International Symposium on Intelligent Control, Munich, Germany, Oct. 2006.

[29] P. Ascencio, D. Sbarbaro, S. Feyo de Azebedo, An adaptive fuzzy hybrid state observer for bioprocesses, IEEE Transactions on Fuzzy Systems 12 (5) (2004) 641–665.

[30] G. Bastin, D. Dochain, On-line estimation and adaptive control of bioreactors, Chemical Engineering Science 46 (11) (1991).

[31] I. Chairez, A. Cabrera, A. Pozniak, T. Pozniak, A continuous time neuro-observer for human immunodeficiency virus (HIV) dynamics, in: Proceedings of the 15th IFAC World Congress, vol. 15, 2002.

[32] D. Kirschner, Using mathematics to understand HIV immune dynamics, Notices of the American Mathematical Society 43 (1996) 51–60.

[33] A.Y. Alanis, E.N. Sanchez, E.A. Hernandez, Reduced neural observers for a class of MIMO discrete-time nonlinear system, in: Proceedings of 2009 6th International Conference on Electrical Engineering, Computing Science and Automatic Control, vol. 1, no. 1, 2009, pp. 1–6.

[34] E.A. Hernandez-Vargas, A.Y. Alanis, E.N. Sanchez, Discrete-time neural observer for HIV infection dynamics, in: World Automation Congress Proceedings, 2012, Art. No. 6320891.

[35] A.Y. Alanis, M. Hernandez-Gonzalez, E.A. Hernandez-Vargas, Observers for biological systems, Applied Soft Computing 24 (2014) 1175–1182.

[36] E.N. Sanchez, D. Urrego, A.Y. Alanis, S. Carlos-Hernandez, Recurrent higher order neural observers for anaerobic processes, in: Artificial Higher Order Neural Networks for Computer Science and Engineering, Idea Group Inc., ISBN 9781615207114, Feb. 2010.

[37] P. Ascencio, D. Sbarbaro, S. Feyo de Azebedo, An adaptive fuzzy hybrid state observer for bioprocesses, IEEE Transactions on Fuzzy Systems 12 (5) (2004) 641–665.

[38] G. Bastin, D. Dochain, On-line estimation and adaptive control of bioreactors, Chemical Engineering Science 46 (11) (1991).

[39] S. Carlos-Hernandez, J.F. Beteau, E.N. Sanchez, Design and real-time implementation of a TS fuzzy observer for anaerobic wastewater treatment plants, in: IEEE International Symposium on Intelligent Control, Munich, Germany, Oct. 2006.

[40] K.J. Gurubel, A.Y. Alanis, E.N. Sanchez, S. Carlos-Hernandez, A neural observer with time-varying learning rate: analysis and applications, International Journal of Neural Systems 24 (1) (2014) 1450011.

[41] E.A. Hernandez-Vargas, A.Y. Alanis, E.N. Sanchez, M. Hernandez-Gonzalez, V. Flores, Supervisor difuso funcional aplicado a una planta urbana de tratamiento de aguas residuales basado en un observador neuronal, Ingenieria Química 36 (Nov. 2009) 14–22.

[42] WHO, Data and Statistics, Global Summary of the Aids Epidemic, The World Health Organization, 2009, http://www.who.int/hiv/data/en/index.html.

[43] H. Hernandez-Vargas, P. Colaneri, R.H. Middleton, Switching strategies to mitigate HIV mutation, IEEE Transactions on Control Systems Technology 22 (2013) 1623–1628.

[44] X. Xiaohua, Estimation of HIV/AIDS parameters, Automatica 39 (2003) 1983–1984.

[45] I. Chairez, A. Cabrera, A. Pozniak, T. Pozniak, A continuous time neuro observer for human immunodeficiency virus (HIV) dynamics, in: Proceedings of the 15th IFAC World Congress, vol. 15, 2002.

[46] D. Campos-Delgado, E. Palacios, Non-linear observer for the estimation of CD8 count under HIV-1 infection, in: American Control Conference, 2007, pp. 4101–4105.

[47] H. Chang, A. Astolfi, Enhancement of the immune system in HIV dynamics by output feedback, Automatica 45 (7) (2009) 1765–1770.

[48] J. David, H. Tran, H.T. Banks, Receding horizon control of HIV, Optimal Control Applications & Methods (2010).

[49] R. Zurakowski, Nonlinear observer output-feedback MPC treatment scheduling for HIV, BioMedical Engineering Online 10 (2011).

CHAPTER 4

Reduced Order Neural Observers

ABSTRACT

This chapter presents the reduced order neural observers for discrete-time nonlinear systems with linear or nonlinear outputs. The applicability of such observers is shown with real-time implementations for electromechanical and biological systems.

KEYWORDS

Reduced order observers

Neural observers

Unknown discrete-time nonlinear systems

Human immunodeficiency virus (HIV)

Rotatory induction motors

Linear induction motors

4.1 REDUCED ORDER OBSERVERS

The approaches, mentioned in the previous chapters, estimate the full state, including the measurable variables. In order to reduce computational complexity, in this chapter we propose the use of a reduced order neural observer, which uses the available measurement and estimates only the unmeasurable variables; furthermore, this observer provides mathematical models for unknown nonlinear systems. The main difference between the previously designed full order neural observer and the reduced one, proposed in this chapter, is the use of the available plant measurements for the design of a series–parallel observer instead of a parallel one, as designed in Chapter 3.

In this chapter, we consider the same class of MIMO discrete-time nonlinear system used in Chapter 3, for which we develop a reduced order Luenberger-like observer [3]; then this observer is applied to a discrete-time unknown nonlinear system [4]. This observer is based on a recurrent high order neural network (RHONN) [10], which estimates the state vector of the unknown plant

75

Discrete-Time Neural Observers. DOI: 10.1016/B978-0-12-810543-6.00004-6

dynamics. The learning algorithm for the RHONN is based on an extended Kalman filter (EKF). For measurable state variables, the RHONN is designed as an identifier [9], while for the non-measurable state variables the RHONN is developed along the lines of the neural observer proposed in Chapter 3. This combination improves the neural observer performance and substantially reduces computational complexity.

4.2   NEURAL IDENTIFIERS

Due to the fact that the reduced order neural observer requires the use of a neural identifier for the measurable variables, in this section we briefly review this topic. Consider the problem of identifying the nonlinear system

$$\chi(k+1) = F(\chi(k), u(k)) \tag{4.1}$$

where $\chi \in \Re^n$, $u \in \Re^m$, and $F \in \Re^n \times \Re^m \to \Re^n$ is a nonlinear function. To identify system (4.1), we use an RHONN defined as

$$x_i(k+1) = w_i^\top z_i(x(k), \varrho(k)), \quad i = 1, \dots, n. \tag{4.2}$$

The RHONN identifier is trained with the EKF (3.8). The identification error can be defined as

$$e_i(k) = \chi_i(k) - x_i(k) \tag{4.3}$$

whose dynamics can be expressed by

$$e_i(k+1) = \widetilde{w}_i(k) z_i(x(k), u(k)) + \epsilon_{z_i}. \tag{4.4}$$

On the other hand, the dynamics of the weight estimation error (2.14) is

$$\widetilde{w}_i(k+1) = \widetilde{w}_i(k) - \eta_i K_i(k) e(k). \tag{4.5}$$

To this end, we establish the following theorem.

Theorem 4.1. *The RHONN (4.2) trained with the modified EKF-based algorithm (3.8) to identify the nonlinear plant (4.1) ensures that the identification error (4.3) is semi-globally uniformly ultimately bounded (SGUUB); moreover, the RHONN weights remain bounded.*

Proof. This proof is along the same lines as the one of Theorem 3.1, the identifier being a special case of the neural observer with $C = I$, where I is an identity matrix.   □

4.3   LINEAR OUTPUT CASE

Many of nonlinear control publications assume complete accessibility to the system state, which is not always possible. For this reason, nonlinear state estimation is a very important topic for nonlinear control [1]. State estimation has been studied by many authors who have obtained interesting results in different directions. Most of those results estimate the whole state, including the measurable variables. In order to reduce the computational complexity, in this section we propose the use of a reduced order neural observer, which uses the available variables and estimates only the unmeasurable ones; moreover, the proposed observer builds mathematical models for unknown nonlinear systems.

The full state observer adds n first-order difference equations to the n equations corresponding to the system model, and thus doubles the respective complexity. If each component of the measurement $y(t)$ is independent of the others (i.e., if C has full rank p), then we really need to estimate only $r = n - p$ components of the system state. We start by considering the special case where the y components correspond to x components. Without loss of generality, we may order the states such that

$$y(k) = Cx(k) = \begin{pmatrix} x_1(k) \\ x_2(k) \\ \vdots \\ x_p(k) \end{pmatrix}$$

with $C = \left[I_p 0_{p \times (n-p)} \right]$, $x \in \Re^n$, $y \in \Re^p$. It is convenient to define

$$x_a(k) = \begin{pmatrix} x_1(k) \\ \vdots \\ x_p(k) \end{pmatrix},$$

$$x_b(k) = \begin{pmatrix} x_{p+1}(k) \\ \vdots \\ x_n(k) \end{pmatrix}$$

with x_a being the measured variables and x_b the unmeasured ones.

Then the complete equations can be written as

$$\begin{pmatrix} x_a(k+1) \\ x_b(k+1) \end{pmatrix} = \begin{pmatrix} f_a(x_a(k), x_b(k), u(k)) \\ f_b(x_a(k), x_b(k), u(k)) \end{pmatrix},$$

$$y(k) = \left[I_p, 0_{p \times r} \right] \begin{pmatrix} x_a(k) \\ x_b(k) \end{pmatrix}.$$

Component-wise, the state equations are

$$x_a(k+1) = f_a(x_a(k), x_b(k), u(k)) + d_a(k),$$
$$x_b(k+1) = f_b(x_a(k), x_b(k), u(k)) + d_b(k),$$
$$y(k) = x_a(k), \tag{4.6}$$

where $u(k) \in \Re^m$ is the input vector, $f_a(\bullet)$ and $f_b(\bullet)$ are unknown nonlinear functions, and $d(k) = [\ d_a(k) \quad d_a(k)\ ]^\top \in \Re^n$ is a disturbance vector. Then, as

x_a are the measurable variables, it is only necessary to design an observer for x_b; notice that the dimension of the observer dynamic equations is $r = n - p$. For this reason, it is referred to as a *reduced order observer* [6].

As explained above, $f_a(\bullet)$ and $f_b(\bullet)$ are unknown nonlinear functions, for which x_a are the measurable variables and x_b are the unmeasurable ones. Hence, in this section, we consider a neural identifier for x_a and a neural observer to estimate x_b for system (4.6) which is assumed to be observable.

For system (4.6), we propose a reduced order neural observer (RONO) with the following structure:

$$\widehat{x}(k) = \begin{bmatrix} \widehat{x}_1(k) \ldots & \widehat{x}_n(k) \end{bmatrix}^\top,$$
$$\widehat{x}_i(k+1) = w_i^\top z_i(x_a(k), \widehat{x}_b(k)u(k)) + g_i e(k),$$
$$\widehat{x}_j(k+1) = w_j^\top z_j(x_a(k), u(k)) + g_j e(k),$$
$$\widehat{y}(k) = C\widehat{x}(k) \tag{4.7}$$

with

$$x_a(k) = \begin{bmatrix} x_1(k) & \ldots & x_i(k) & \ldots & x_p(k) \end{bmatrix},$$
$$\widehat{x}_b(k) = \begin{bmatrix} \widehat{x}_{p+1}(k) & \ldots & \widehat{x}_j(k) & \ldots & \widehat{x}_n(k) \end{bmatrix},$$

and $i = 1, \ldots, p$, $j = p+1, \ldots, n$, $g_i, g_j \in \Re^p$, w_i, w_j, z_i, and z_j as in (2.7); the weight vectors are updated online with a decoupled EKF (3.8), the output error is defined by

$$e(k) = y(k) - \widehat{y}(k), \tag{4.8}$$

and the state estimation error as

$$\widetilde{x}(k) = x(k) - \widehat{x}(k). \tag{4.9}$$

Considering (4.8) and (4.9), we get

$$e(k) = C\widetilde{x}(k). \tag{4.10}$$

Hence, the dynamics of $x_i(k+1)$ can be expressed as

$$\widetilde{x}_i(k+1) = x_i(k+1) - \widehat{x}_i(k+1). \tag{4.11}$$

Then

$$\widetilde{x}_i(k+1) = w_i^{*\top} z_i(x(k), u(k)) + \epsilon_{z_i}$$
$$- w_i^\top(k) z_i(x_a(k), \widehat{x}_b(k), u(k)) - g_i e(k). \tag{4.12}$$

Adding and subtracting $w_i^{*\top} z_i(x_a(k), \widehat{x}_b(k)u(k))$, (4.12) can be written as

$$\widetilde{x}_i(k+1) = \widetilde{w}_i^\top(k) z_i(x_a(k), \widehat{x}_b(k), u(k)) + \epsilon'_{z_i} - g_i e(k) \tag{4.13}$$

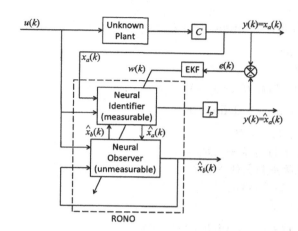

FIGURE 4.1 Reduced order neural observer scheme for the linear output case.

with

$$\epsilon'_{z_i} = w_i^{*\top} z_i (\widetilde{x}(k), u(k)) + \epsilon_{z_i},$$ (4.14)
$$z_i (\widetilde{x}(k), u(k)) = z_i (x(k), u(k)) - z_i (x_a(k), \widehat{x}_b(k), u(k)).$$

It is clear from (4.14) that ϵ'_{z_i} is bounded since ϵ_{z_i} and $z_i (\widetilde{x}(k), u(k))$ terms are individually bounded above [1]. On the other hand, the dynamics of $x_j (k + 1)$ can be expressed as

$$\widetilde{x}_j (k + 1) = x_j (k + 1) - \widehat{x}_j (k + 1),$$ (4.15)
$$\widetilde{x}_j (k + 1) = \widetilde{w}_j^\top (k) z_j(x_a(k), u(k)) + \epsilon'_{z_j} - g_j e (k),$$ (4.16)

with

$$\epsilon'_{z_j} = w_j^{*\top} z_j (\widetilde{x}(k), u(k)) + \epsilon_{z_j},$$ (4.17)
$$z_j (\widetilde{x}(k), u(k)) = z_j (x(k), u(k)) - z_j (x_a(k), u(k)).$$

It is clear from (4.14) that ϵ'_{z_j} is bounded since ϵ_{z_j} and $z_j (\widetilde{x}(k), u(k))$ terms are individually bounded above [1]. Furthermore, the dynamics of (2.14) is

$$\widetilde{w}_i (k + 1) = \widetilde{w}_i (k) - \eta_i K_i (k) e (k), \quad i = 1, 2, \ldots, n.$$ (4.18)

The proposed reduced order neural observer scheme is shown in Fig. 4.1.

Considering (3.8) and (4.6)–(4.18), we establish the first main result of this chapter as the following theorem.

Theorem 4.2. *For system (4.6), the RONO (4.7), trained with the EKF-based algorithm (3.8), ensures that the estimation error (4.9) and the output error (4.10) are semi-globally uniformly ultimately bounded (SGUUB); moreover, the RONO weights remain bounded.*

Proof. Consider the component-wise form of a Lyapunov function candidate.

Case 1. Measurable variables. For x_i with $i = 1, \ldots, p$, consider the Lyapunov function candidate

$$V_i(k) = \widetilde{w}_i(k) P_i(k) \widetilde{w}_i(k) + \widetilde{x}_i(k) \widetilde{x}_i(k) \tag{4.19}$$

whose first increment is defined as

$$
\begin{aligned}
\Delta V_i(k) &= V(k+1) - V(k) \\
&= \widetilde{w}_i(k+1) P_i(k+1) \widetilde{w}_i(k+1) \\
&\quad + \widetilde{x}_i(k+1) \widetilde{x}_i(k+1) \\
&\quad - \widetilde{w}_i(k) P_i(k) \widetilde{w}_i(k) \\
&\quad - \widetilde{x}_i(k) \widetilde{x}_i(k).
\end{aligned}
\tag{4.20}
$$

Using (3.8) and (4.18) in (4.20), we obtain

$$
\begin{aligned}
\Delta V_i(k) &= \left[\widetilde{w}_i(k) - \eta_i K_i(k) e(k)\right]^T [A_i(k)]\left[\widetilde{w}_i(k) - \eta_i K_i(k) e(k)\right] \\
&\quad + \left[f(k) - g_i C\widetilde{x}(k)\right]^T [A_i(k)]\left[f(k) - g_i C\widetilde{x}(k)\right] \\
&\quad - \widetilde{w}_i(k) P_i(k) \widetilde{w}_i(k) - \widetilde{x}_i(k) P_i(k) \widetilde{x}_i(k) \\
&= -\widetilde{w}_i^T(k) B_i(k) \widetilde{w}_i(k) - \eta_i \widetilde{x}^T(k) C^T K_i^T(k) A_i(k) \widetilde{w}_i(k) \\
&\quad - \eta_i \widetilde{w}_i^T(k) A_i(k) C\widetilde{x}(k) + \eta_i^2 \widetilde{x}^T(k) C^T K_i^T(k) A_i(k) K_i(k) C\widetilde{x}(k) \\
&\quad + f^T(k) f(k) - f^T(k) g_i C\widetilde{x}(k) - \widetilde{x}^T(k) C^T g_i^T f(k) \\
&\quad + \widetilde{x}^T(k) C^T g_i^T g_i C\widetilde{x}(k) - \widetilde{x}_i^T(k) \widetilde{x}_i(k),
\end{aligned}
\tag{4.21}
$$

with

$$A_i(k) = P_i(k) - B_i(k),$$
$$B_i(k) = K_i(k) H_i^\top(k) P_i(k) + Q_i(k),$$
$$f_i(k) = \widetilde{w}_i(k) z_i(x_a(k), \widehat{x}_b(k), u(k)) + \epsilon_{z_i}'.$$

Using the following inequalities:

$$X^T X + Y^T Y \ge -X^T Y - Y^T X,$$
$$-\lambda_{\min}(P) X^2 \ge -X^T P X \ge -\lambda_{\max}(P) X^2,$$

which are valid $\forall X, Y \in \Re^n$, $\forall P \in \Re^{n \times n}$, $P = P^T > 0$, expression (4.21) can be written as

$$
\begin{aligned}
\Delta V_i(k) &\le -\|\widetilde{w}_i(k)\|^2 \lambda_{\min}(B_i(k)) + 2\|f_i(k)\|^2 \\
&\quad + \eta_i^2 \|\widetilde{x}(k)\|^2 \|C\|^2 \|K_i(k)\|^2 \lambda_{\max} A_i(k) \\
&\quad + 2\|\widetilde{x}(k)\|^2 \|C\|^2 \|g_i\|^2 - \|\widetilde{x}(k)\|^2 \\
&\quad + \|K_i(k)\|^2 \|A_i(k)\|^2 \|\widetilde{w}_i(k)\|^2 + \eta_i^2 \|\widetilde{x}(k)\|^2 \|C\|^2.
\end{aligned}
\tag{4.22}
$$

Substituting $f_i(k) = \widetilde{w}_i(k) z_i(x_a(k), \widehat{x}_b(k), u(k)) + \epsilon_{z_i}'$ in (4.22) yields

$$\Delta V_i(k) \le -\|\widetilde{w}_i(k)\|^2 \lambda_{\min}(B_i(k)) + 2\|\widetilde{w}_i(k)\|^2 \|z_i(x_a(k), \widehat{x}_b(k), u(k))\|^2$$

$$+ \eta_i^2 \| \widetilde{x}(k) \|^2 \| C \|^2 \| K_i(k) \|^2 \lambda_{\max} A_i(k)$$
$$+ 2 \| \widetilde{x}(k) \|^2 \| C \|^2 \| g_i \|^2 - \| \widetilde{x}(k) \|^2 + \eta_i^2 \| \widetilde{x}(k) \|^2 \| C \|^2$$
$$+ \| K_i(k) \|^2 \| A_i(k) \|^2 \| \widetilde{w}_i(k) \|^2 + 2 \left| \epsilon'_{z_i} \right|^2. \tag{4.23}$$

Defining

$$E_i(k) = \lambda_{\min}(B_i(k)) - \| K_i(k) \|^2 \| A_i(k) \|^2 - 2 \| z_i(x_a(k), \widehat{x}_b(k), u(k)) \|^2, \tag{4.24}$$
$$F_i(k) = 1 - \eta_i^2 \| C \|^2 \| K_i(k) \|^2 \lambda_{\max} A_i(k) - 2 \| C \|^2 \| g_i \|^2 - \eta_i^2 \| C \|^2, \tag{4.25}$$

inequality (4.23) can be rewritten as

$$\Delta V_i(k) \le - \| \widetilde{w}_i(k) \|^2 E_i(k) - \| \widetilde{x}(k) \|^2 F_i(k) + 2 \left| \epsilon'_{z_i} \right|^2.$$

Hence, $\Delta V_i(k) \le 0$ whenever

$$\| \widetilde{x}(k) \|^2 > \sqrt{\frac{2 \left| \epsilon'_{z_i} \right|^2}{F_i(k)}}$$

or

$$\| \widetilde{w}_i(k) \|^2 > \sqrt{\frac{2 \left| \epsilon'_{z_i} \right|^2}{E_i(k)}}.$$

Therefore, the solution of (4.11) and (4.18) is SGUUB, hence the estimation error and the RONO weights are SGUUB [2].

Case 2. Unmeasurable variables. For x_j with $j = p + 1, \ldots, n$, consider the Lyapunov function candidate

$$V_j(k) = \widetilde{w}_j(k) P_j(k) \widetilde{w}_j(k) + \widetilde{x}_j(k) \widetilde{x}_j(k). \tag{4.26}$$

Using (3.8) and (4.18), its first difference can be expressed as

$$\Delta V_j(k) = - \widetilde{w}_j^T(k) B_j(k) \widetilde{w}_j(k) - \eta_j \widetilde{x}^T(k) C^T K_j^T(k) A_j(k) \widetilde{w}_j(k)$$
$$- \eta_j \widetilde{w}_j^T(k) A_j(k) C \widetilde{x}(k) + \eta_j^2 \widetilde{x}^T(k) C^T K_j^T(k) A_i(k) K_j(k) C \widetilde{x}(k)$$
$$+ f_j^T(k) f_j(k) - f_j^T(k) g_j C \widetilde{x}(k) - \widetilde{x}^T(k) C^T g_j^T f_j(k)$$
$$+ \widetilde{x}^T(k) C^T g_j^T g_j C \widetilde{x}(k) - \widetilde{x}_j^T(k) \widetilde{x}_j(k), \tag{4.27}$$

with

$$A_j(k) = P_j(k) - B_j(k),$$
$$B_j(k) = K_j(k) H_j^T(k) P_j(k) + Q_j(k),$$
$$f_j(k) = \widetilde{w}_j(k) z_j(x_a(k), \widehat{x}_b(k), u(k)) + \epsilon'_{z_j}.$$

As in *Case 1*,

$$\Delta V_j(k) \le - \| \widetilde{w}_j(k) \|^2 \lambda_{\min}(B_j(k)) + 2 \| \widetilde{w}_j(k) \|^2 \| z_j(x_a(k), \widehat{x}_b(k), u(k)) \|^2$$
$$+ \eta_j^2 \| \widetilde{x}(k) \|^2 \| C \|^2 \| K_j(k) \|^2 \lambda_{\max} A_j(k)$$

$$+ 2 \|\widetilde{x}(k)\|^2 \|C\|^2 \|g_j\|^2 - \|\widetilde{x}(k)\|^2 + \eta_j^2 \|\widetilde{x}(k)\|^2 \|C\|^2$$
$$+ \|K_j(k)\|^2 \|A_j(k)\|^2 \|\widetilde{w}_j(k)\|^2 + 2 \left|\epsilon'_{z_j}\right|^2. \tag{4.28}$$

Defining

$$E_j(k) = \lambda_{\min}\left(B_j(k)\right) - \|K_j(k)\|^2 \|A_j(k)\|^2 - 2 \|z_j(x_a(k), \widehat{x}_b(k), u(k))\|^2, \tag{4.29}$$

$$F_j(k) = 1 - \eta_j^2 \|C\|^2 \|K_j(k)\|^2 \lambda_{\max} A_j(k) - 2 \|C\|^2 \|g_j\|^2 - \eta_j^2 \|C\|^2, \tag{4.30}$$

inequality (4.28) can be rewritten as

$$\Delta V_j(k) \leq - \|\widetilde{w}_j(k)\|^2 E_j(k) - \|\widetilde{x}(k)\|^2 F_j(k) + 2 \left|\epsilon'_{z_j}\right|^2.$$

Hence, $\Delta V_j(k) \leq 0$ whenever

$$\|\widetilde{x}(k)\|^2 > \sqrt{\frac{2 \left|\epsilon'_{z_j}\right|^2}{F_j(k)}}$$

or

$$\|\widetilde{w}_j(k)\|^2 > \sqrt{\frac{2 \left|\epsilon'_{z_j}\right|^2}{E_j(k)}}.$$

Therefore, the solution of (4.15) and (4.18) is SGUUB, hence the estimation error and the RONO weights are SGUUB [2].

To finish the proof, consider the Lyapunov function candidate and its increment:

$$V(k) = \sum_{i=1}^{n} \widetilde{w}_i^T(k) P_i(k) \widetilde{w}_i(k) + \widetilde{x}_i(k) \widetilde{x}_i(k), \tag{4.31}$$

$$\Delta V(k) = \sum_{i=1}^{n} \left(\widetilde{w}_i^T(k+1) P_i(k+1) \widetilde{w}_i(k+1) + \widetilde{x}_i(k+1) \widetilde{x}_i(k+1) \right.$$
$$\left. - \widetilde{w}_i^T(k) P_i(k) \widetilde{w}_i(k) - \widetilde{x}_i(k) \widetilde{x}_i(k) \right).$$

Therefore, as above, (4.31) can be expressed as

$$\Delta V(k) \leq \sum_{i=1}^{n} \left(- \|\widetilde{w}_i(k)\|^2 E_i(k) - \|\widetilde{x}(k)\|^2 F_i(k) + 2 \left|\epsilon'_{z_i}\right|^2 \right)$$

with

$$E_i(k) = \lambda_{\min}\left(B_i(k)\right) - \|K_i(k)\|^2 \|A_i(k)\|^2 - 2 \|z_i(x_a(k), \widehat{x}_b(k), u(k))\|^2,$$
$$F_i(k) = 1 - \eta_i^2 \|C\|^2 \|K_i(k)\|^2 \lambda_{\max} A_i(k) - 2 \|C\|^2 \|g_i\|^2 - \eta_i^2 \|C\|^2.$$

As a result, $\Delta V(k) \leq 0$ whenever

$$\|\tilde{x}(k)\|^2 > \sqrt{\frac{2\left|\epsilon'_{z_i}\right|^2}{F_i(k)}} \equiv \kappa_1$$

or

$$\|\tilde{w}_i(k)\|^2 > \sqrt{\frac{2\left|\epsilon'_{z_i}\right|^2}{E_i(k)}} \equiv \kappa_2,$$

and if $\|\tilde{x}(k)\| > \kappa_1$ or $\|\tilde{w}_i(k)\| > \kappa_2$, $\forall i = 1, \ldots, n$ holds, then $\Delta V(k) \leq 0$.

Finally, from (4.10) it is easy too see that the output error has an algebraic relation with $\tilde{x}(k)$; for that reason, if $\tilde{x}(k)$ is bounded $e(k)$ is bounded, too:

$$e(k) = C\tilde{x}(k),$$
$$\|e(k)\| = \|C\| \|\tilde{x}(k)\|.$$

$\square$

4.4 NONLINEAR OUTPUT CASE

Using the well-known approximation capabilities of neural networks, neural observers have emerged [4,11–15]; one of the main advantages of this kind of observers is its robustness to uncertainties, external disturbances, among others. In [16–21], neural observers are designed to estimate the state for continuous-time nonlinear systems. Although discrete-time observers are preferred for real time applications, the discrete-time case has not been exploited as the continuous one. In [15,22], neural observers are proposed to estimate the state for discrete-time nonlinear systems. However, several approaches mentioned above need the previous knowledge of the plant model at least partially [17–22]. The problem of unknown model dynamics are considered in [15,16,23–25], considering only the presence of external disturbances. The main disadvantage of these schemes is that they can only work for systems with linear outputs. There are real-life applications where the output is a nonlinear combination of the state variables [26,27]. These works tackle the estimation problem for systems with nonlinear outputs. Nevertheless, previous knowledge of the model and parameters is required.

Now, the RONO for discrete-time nonlinear systems with nonlinear outputs is proposed [7,8]; as in the previous section, without loss of generality, we may order the states such that

$$y(k) = h(x_a(k))$$

with h a known, invertible nonlinear map, which for analytic purposes is considered Lipschitz, $p + r = n$, $x \in \Re^n$, $y \in \Re^p$. Then the complete equations can be written as

$$\begin{pmatrix} x_a(k+1) \\ x_b(k+1) \end{pmatrix} = \begin{pmatrix} f_a(x_a(k), x_b(k), u(k)) \\ f_b(x_a(k), x_b(k), u(k)) \end{pmatrix},$$
$$y(k) = h(x_a(k)).$$

Component-wise, the state equations are

$$x_a(k+1) = f_a(x_a(k), x_b(k), u(k)) + d_a(k),$$
$$x_b(k+1) = f_b(x_a(k), x_b(k), u(k)) + d_b(k),$$
$$y(k) = h(x_a(k)) \tag{4.32}$$

with $x_a(k)$, $x_b(k)$, $u(k)$, $f_a(\bullet)$, $f_b(\bullet)$, $d(k)$ defined as in previous section. Then,

$$x_a(k) = h^{-1}(y(k)).$$

As explained above, $f_a(\bullet)$ and $f_b(\bullet)$ are unknown nonlinear functions, for which x_a are the measurable variables and x_b are the unmeasurable ones. Hence, in this section, we consider a neural identifier for x_a and a neural observer to estimate x_b for system (4.6) which is assumed to be observable.

For system (4.6), we propose a reduced order neural observer (RONO) with the following structure:

$$\hat{x}(k) = \begin{bmatrix} \hat{x}_1(k) & \dots & \hat{x}_n(k) \end{bmatrix}^{\mathsf{T}},$$
$$\hat{x}_i(k+1) = w_i^{\mathsf{T}} z_i(x_a(k), \hat{x}_b(k)u(k)) + g_i e(k),$$
$$\hat{x}_j(k+1) = w_j^{\mathsf{T}} z_j(x_a(k), u(k)) + g_j e(k),$$
$$\hat{y}(k) = h(\hat{x}_a(k)), \tag{4.33}$$

with

$$x_a(k) = \begin{bmatrix} x_1(k) & \dots & x_i(k) & \dots & x_p(k) \end{bmatrix},$$
$$\hat{x}_b(k) = \begin{bmatrix} \hat{x}_{p+1}(k) & \dots & \hat{x}_j(k) & \dots & \hat{x}_n(k) \end{bmatrix},$$

and $i = 1, \dots, p$, $j = p+1, \dots, n$, $g_i, g_j \in \Re^p$, w_i, w_j, z_i, and z_j as in (2.7); the weight vectors are updated online with a decoupled EKF (3.8), the output error, the state estimation error and their respective dynamics defined as in the previous section.

The proposed reduced order neural observer scheme is shown in Fig. 4.2.

Considering (3.8) and (4.6)–(4.18), we establish the second main result of this chapter as the following theorem.

Theorem 4.3. *For system (4.6), the RONO (4.7), trained with the EKF-based algorithm (3.8), ensures that the estimation error (4.9) and the output error (4.10) are semi-globally uniformly ultimately bounded (SGUUB); moreover, the RONO weights remain bounded.*

Proof. Considering that $h(\cdot)$ is a Lipschitz function, the proof can be conducted in the same way as the proof of Theorem 4.2, with $\|h(x_a(k)) - h(\hat{x}_a(k))\| \leq L \|x_a(k) - \hat{x}_a(k)\|$, where L is the Lipschitz constant, as in Theorem 3.2.   □

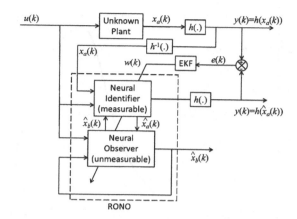

FIGURE 4.2 Reduced order neural observer scheme for nonlinear output case.

4.5 APPLICATIONS

To illustrate the applicability of the above proposed RONO, in this section four meaningful application are presented. The proposed RONO (4.7) is applied in simulation of the van der Pol system and the HIV; then the same RONO is implemented in real-time for rotatory induction motors and linear induction ones. All RONOs are trained online with an EKF-learning algorithm (3.8) under the assumption that the plant models are unknown, as are external disturbances and parameter variations.

4.5.1 van der Pol System

In this section, the neural observer is applied to a modified van der Pol oscillator, whose nonlinear dynamics is represented by the following equation [5]:

$$x_1 (k + 1) = x_1 (k) + T x_2 (k),$$
$$x_2 (k + 1) = x_2 (k) + T \left(\xi \left(0.5 - x_1^2 (k) \right) x_2 (k) \right)$$
$$\qquad + T \left(-x_1 (k) + u (k) \right),$$
$$y (k) = x_1 (k),$$
$$u (k) = 0.5 \cos (1.1 k T), \tag{4.34}$$

where variables $x \in \mathfrak{R}^2$, $u \in \mathfrak{R}$, and $y \in \mathfrak{R}$ are the state, input, and output of the system, respectively, and T is the sampling period, which is fixed at 1×10^{-3} s, and ξ is a parameter whose nominal value is equal to 1; however, for this application such a parameter is considered as time-varying (which is assumed unknown), during the state estimation process.

In this application, x_1 is the measurable state, thus an identifier is used to estimate its dynamics. x_2 is the unmeasurable state, therefore, it is necessary to

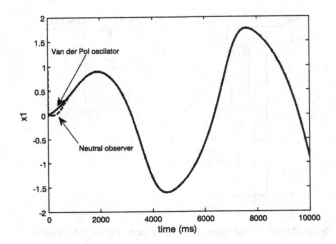

FIGURE 4.3 Time evolution of the state $x_1(k)$ (solid line) and its estimate $\widehat{x}_1(k)$ (dashed line).

use an RONO to estimate both its value and dynamics. Then to estimate the state x_2, we use the RONO (4.7) with $n = 2$ trained with the EKF (3.8):

$$
\begin{aligned}
\widehat{x}_1(k+1) ={}& w_{11}(k)\, S(\widehat{x}_2(k))\, S(u(k)) \\
& + w_{12}(k)\, S^2(\widehat{x}_2(k))\, S(x_1(k))\, S^2(u(k)) \\
& + w_{13}(k)\, S(x_1(k)) + g_1 e(k), \\
\widehat{x}_2(k+1) ={}& w_{21}(k)\, S(x_1(k))\, S(\widehat{x}_2(k))\, S(u(k)) \\
& + w_{22}(k)\, S(u(k))\, S(\widehat{x}_2(k)) \\
& + w_{23}(k)\, S(u(k))\, S^2(\widehat{x}_2(k)) + g_2 e(k), \\
\widehat{y}(k) ={}& \widehat{x}_1(k).
\end{aligned}
\tag{4.35}
$$

The training is performed online, using a parallel configuration as displayed in Fig. 4.2. All the NN states are initialized in a random way. The associated covariance matrices are initialized as diagonals, and the nonzero elements are: $P_1(0) = P_2(0) = 100{,}000$, $Q_1(0) = Q_2(0) = 1000$, and $R_1(0) = R_2(0) = 10{,}000$, respectively. The simulation results are presented in Figs. 4.3 and 4.4. They display the time evolution of the estimated states $x_1(k)$ and $x_2(k)$, respectively. Fig. 4.5 shows the estimation errors.

4.5.2 RONO for the HIV Model

In this section, the neural observer is applied to an HIV model (3.38). The RONO is applied to HIV dynamics which is considered unknown. To estimate the number of viral cells in the blood stream ($V = x_3$) with the online concentration of infected cells ($T^i = x_2$) as well as uninfected ($T = x_1$) ones, we use a sampling time of 20 minutes. Then in this application the neural identifier

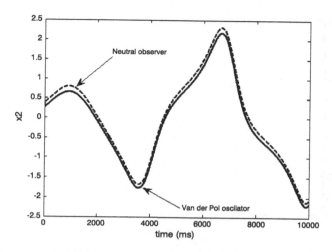

FIGURE 4.4 Time evolution of the state $x_2(k)$ (solid line) and its estimate $\widehat{x}_2(k)$ (dashed line).

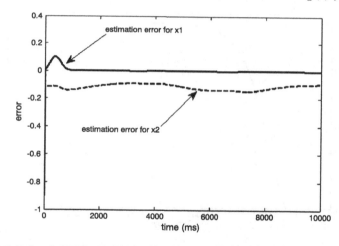

FIGURE 4.5 Estimation errors $\widetilde{x}_1(k)$ (solid line) and $\widetilde{x}_2(k)$ (dashed line).

is applied to x_1 and x_2, and the RONO is designed for x_3. The neural network used for this state estimation is given by

$$\widehat{x}_1(k+1) = w_{11}(k)\, S(\widehat{x}_3(k))$$
$$+ w_{12}(k)\, S(x_1(k))^2\, S(x_2(k))$$
$$+ w_{13}(k)\, S(x_1(k))\, S(\widehat{x}_3(k))\, S(u(k))$$
$$+ w_{14}(k)\, S(x_1(k))\, S(x_2(k)) + g_1 e(k),$$
$$\widehat{x}_2(k+1) = w_{21}(k)\, x_1(k)\, \widehat{x}_3(k) + w_{22}(k)\, \widehat{x}_2(k)$$
$$+ w_{23}(k)\, S(\widehat{x}_3(k))\, S(u(k))\, x_2(k)\, \widehat{x}_3(k)$$

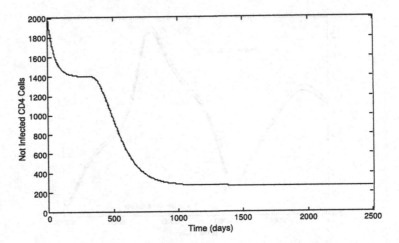

FIGURE 4.6 Time evolution of the state $x_1(k)$ (solid line) and its estimate $\widehat{x}_1(k)$ (dashed line).

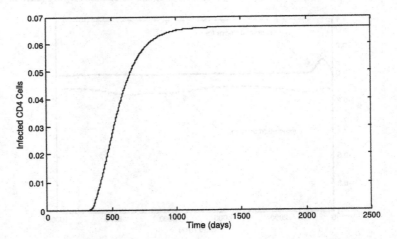

FIGURE 4.7 Time evolution of the state $x_2(k)$ (solid line) and its estimate $\widehat{x}_2(k)$ (dashed line).

$$
\begin{aligned}
&+ g_2 e(k), \\
\widehat{x}_3(k+1) = {}& w_{31}(k)\, S(x_2(k))\, S(\widehat{x}_3(k))\, S(u(k)) \\
&+ w_{32}(k)\, S(x_1(k))\, S(\widehat{x}_3(k)) \\
&+ w_{33}(k)\, S(x_1(k))\, S(\widehat{x}_3(k))^2 + g_2 e(k), \\
\widehat{y}(k) = {}& \begin{bmatrix} \widehat{x}_1(k) & \widehat{x}_2(k) \end{bmatrix}^\top,
\end{aligned}
\tag{4.36}
$$

where $\widehat{x}_1$, $\widehat{x}_2$, and $\widehat{x}_3$ are the estimates for concentration of uninfected cells (T), concentration of infected cells (T^i), and the number of viral cells in the blood stream (V), respectively. The input $u(k) = c$ is the total daily drug dosage in

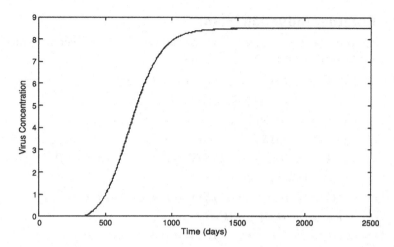

FIGURE 4.8 Time evolution of the state $x_3(k)$ (solid line) and its estimate $\widehat{x}_3(k)$ (dashed line).

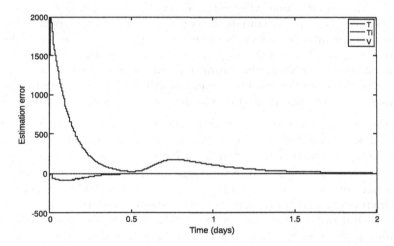

FIGURE 4.9 Estimation errors $\widetilde{x}_1(k)$ (solid black line), $\widetilde{x}_2(k)$ (dashed line), and $\widetilde{x}_3(k)$ (solid gray line).

chemotherapy. The training is performed online, using a parallel configuration as displayed in Fig. 4.1. All the NN states are initialized in a random way. The associated covariance matrices are initialized as diagonals, and the nonzero elements are: $P_1(0) = P_2(0) = P_3(0) = 100{,}000$, $Q_1(0) = Q_2(0) = Q_3(0) = 1000$, $R_1(0) = R_2(0) = R_3(0) = 1000$, respectively, and the Luenberger parameter vector is $g = \begin{bmatrix} 0.2 & 0.01 & 0.0001 \end{bmatrix}^T$. The simulation results are presented in Figs. 4.6, 4.7, and 4.8. They display the time evolution of the estimated states $x_1(k)$, $x_2(k)$, and $x_3(k)$, respectively. Fig. 4.9 shows the estimation errors.

4.5.3 Rotatory Induction Motor

This section presents the reduced order neural network observer as applied to a discrete-time induction motor as follows:

$$
\begin{aligned}
\widehat{x}_1\,(k+1) &= w_{11}\,(k)\,S\,(\omega\,(k)) + w_{12}\,(k)\,S\,(\omega\,(k))\,S\,(\widehat{x}_3\,(k))\,i^\alpha\,(k) \\
&\quad + w_{13}\,(k)\,S\,(\omega\,(k))\,S\,(\widehat{x}_2\,(k))\,i^\beta\,(k) + g_1 e\,(k)\,, \\
\widehat{x}_2\,(k+1) &= w_{21}\,(k)\,S\,(\omega\,(k))\,S\,(\widehat{x}_3\,(k)) + w_{22}\,(k)\,i^\beta\,(k) + g_2 e\,(k)\,, \\
\widehat{x}_3\,(k+1) &= w_{31}\,(k)\,S\,(\omega\,(k))\,S\,(\widehat{x}_2\,(k)) + w_{32}\,(k)\,i^\alpha\,(k) + g_3 e\,(k)\,, \\
\widehat{x}_4\,(k+1) &= w_{41}\,(k)\,S\,(\widehat{x}_2\,(k)) + w_{42}\,(k)\,S\,(\widehat{x}_3\,(k)) + w_{43}\,(k)\,S\,(i^\alpha\,(k)) \\
&\quad + w_{44}\,(k)\,u^\alpha\,(k) + g_4 e\,(k)\,, \\
\widehat{x}_5\,(k+1) &= w_{51}\,(k)\,S\,(\widehat{x}_2\,(k)) + w_{52}\,(k)\,S\,(\widehat{x}_3\,(k)) + w_{53}\,(k)\,S\,(i^\beta\,(k)) \\
&\quad + w_{54}\,(k)\,u^\beta\,(k) + g_5 e\,(k)\,, \\
\widehat{x}_6\,(k+1) &= w_{61}\,(k)\,S\,(\widehat{x}_2\,(k)) + w_{62}\,(k)\,S\,(\widehat{x}_3\,(k)) + w_{63}\,(k)\,S\,(\theta\,(k)) \\
&\quad + g_6 e\,(k)\,,
\end{aligned}
\tag{4.37}
$$

where $\widehat{x}_1$ estimates the angular speed ω; $\widehat{x}_2$ and $\widehat{x}_3$ estimate the fluxes ψ^α and ψ^β, respectively; $\widehat{x}_4$ and $\widehat{x}_5$ estimate the currents i^α and i^β, respectively; finally, $\widehat{x}_6$ estimates the angular displacement θ. The inputs u^α and u^β are selected as chirp functions. The training is performed online, using a parallel configuration. In this application, the neural identifier is designed for x_1, x_4, and x_5, then the RONO is designed for x_2 and x_3. All the NN states are initialized randomly. The associated covariance matrices are initialized as diagonals.

This RONO is applied in real-time to the benchmark described in Section 3.3.2.3. During the estimation process the plant and the NN operate in open-loop. Both of them (plant and NN) have the same input vector $\begin{bmatrix} u_\alpha & u_\beta \end{bmatrix}^\top$; u_α and u_β are chirp functions, with 200 volts of amplitude and incremental frequencies from 0 to 150 Hz and from 0 to 200 Hz, respectively. The implementation is performed with a sampling time of 0.0005 s. The results of the real-time implementation are presented as follows: Fig. 4.10 displays the estimation performance for the speed rotor; Fig. 4.11 and Fig. 4.12 present the estimation performance for the fluxes in phase α and β, respectively. Figs. 4.13 and 4.14 portray the estimation performance for currents in phase α and β, respectively. Finally, Table 4.1 presents the mean value and standard deviation for the state estimation errors.

4.5.4 Linear Induction Motor

For the real-time implementation, a reduced neural observer is proposed as follows:

$$
\begin{aligned}
\hat{x}_1(k+1) &= w_{11}S(q_m(k)) + w_{12}v(k) + g_1 e(k)\,, \\
\hat{x}_2(k+1) &= w_{21}S(v(k)) + w_{22}S(\hat{x}_3(k)) + w_{23}S(\hat{x}_4(k)) + w_{24}S(v(k))S(\hat{x}_4(k)) \\
&\quad + w_{25}S(\hat{x}_3(k))S(\hat{x}_4(k)) + w_{26}S(v(k))S(\hat{x}_3(k))
\end{aligned}
$$

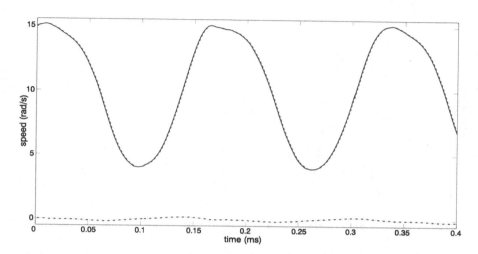

FIGURE 4.10 Real-time rotor speed estimation (plant signal (solid line), neural signal (dashed line), and estimation error (dotted–dashed line)).

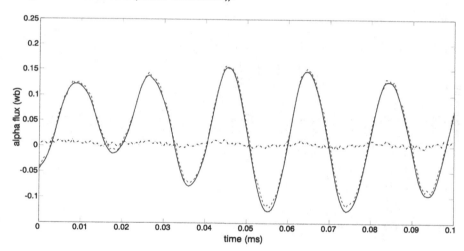

FIGURE 4.11 Real-time alpha flux estimation (plant signal (solid line), neural signal (dashed line), and estimation error (dotted–dashed line)).

$$
- w_v S(\hat{x}_3(k)) \sin(n_p q_m(k)) + S(\hat{x}_4(k)) \cos(n_p q_m(k))) i_\alpha(k)
$$
$$
+ w_v S(\hat{x}_3(k)) \cos(n_p q_m(k)) - S(\hat{x}_4(k)) \sin(n_p q_m(k))) i_\beta(k) + g_2 e(k),
$$
$$
\hat{x}_3(k+1) = w_{31} S(v(k)) + w_{32} S(\hat{x}_3(k)) + w_{33} S(v(k))) S(\hat{x}_3(k))
$$
$$
+ w_{34} S(q_m(k)) S(v(k)) + w_{35} S(q_m(k)) S(\hat{x}_3(k))
$$
$$
+ w_{fa} \cos(n_p q_m(k)) i_\alpha(k) + w_{fa} \sin(n_p q_m(k)) i_\beta(k) + g_3 e(k),
$$
$$
\hat{x}_4(k+1) = w_{41} S(v(k)) + w_{42} S(\hat{x}_4(k)) + w_{43} S(v(k)) S(\hat{x}_4(k))
$$

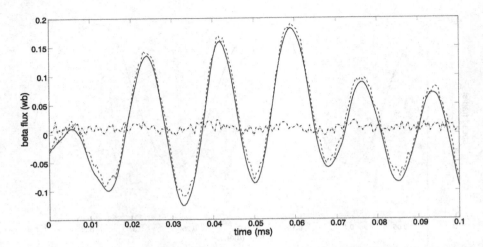

FIGURE 4.12 Real-time beta flux estimation (plant signal (solid line), neural signal (dashed line), and estimation error (dotted–dashed line)).

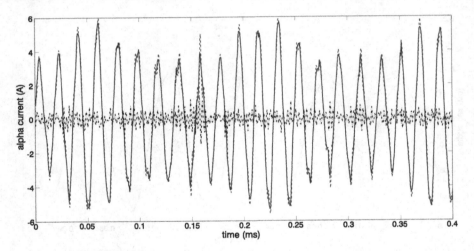

FIGURE 4.13 Real-time alpha current estimation (plant signal (solid line), neural signal (dashed line), and estimation error (dotted–dashed line)).

$$+ w_{44}S(q_m(k))S(v(k)) + w_{45}S(q_m(k))S(\hat{x}_4(k))$$
$$- w_{fa}\sin(n_p q_m(k))i_\alpha(k) + w_{fa}\cos(n_p q_m(k))i_\beta(k) + g_4 e(k),$$
$$\hat{x}_5(k+1) = w_{51}S(v(k)) + w_{52}S(\hat{x}_3(k)) + w_{53}S(\hat{x}_4(k))$$
$$+ w_{54}S(i_\alpha(k)) + w_{55}S(v(k))S(\hat{x}_3(k)) + w_{56}S(v(k))S(\hat{x}_4(k))$$
$$+ w_{57}S(\hat{x}_3(k))S(\hat{x}_4(k)) + w_{58}u_\alpha(k) + g_5 e(k),$$
$$\hat{x}_6(k+1) = w_{61}S(v(k)) + w_{62}S(\hat{x}_3(k)) + w_{63}S(\hat{x}_4(k))$$

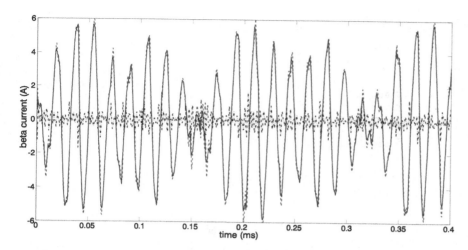

FIGURE 4.14 Real-time beta current estimation (plant signal (solid line), neural signal (dashed line), and estimation error (dotted–dashed line)).

Table 4.1 Standard deviation and mean value for the state estimation error

Variable	Standard Deviation	Mean Value
$\omega - \widehat{x}_1$	0.0876 rad/s	-2.5429×10^{-5} rad/s
$\psi^\alpha - \widehat{x}_2$	0.0019 wb	3.8971×10^{-5} wb
$\psi^\beta - \widehat{x}_3$	0.0021 wb	-4.08234×10^{-5} wb
$i^\alpha - \widehat{x}_4$	0.0257 A	-9.4126×10^{-5} A
$i^\beta - \widehat{x}_5$	0.0314 A	-5.3291×10^{-5} A

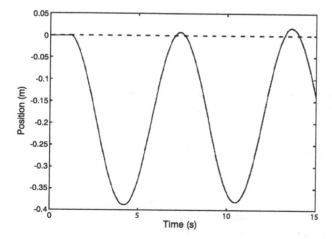

FIGURE 4.15 Real-time position estimation (plant signal (solid line), neural signal (dashed line), and estimation error (dotted–dashed line)).

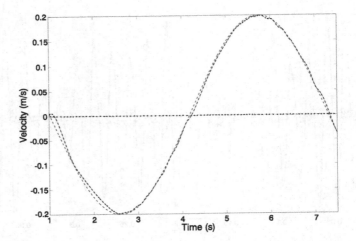

FIGURE 4.16

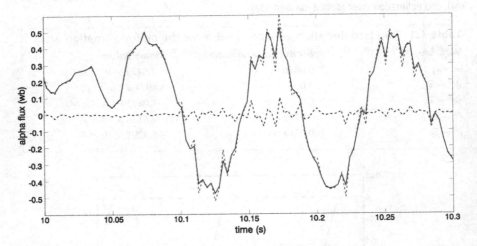

FIGURE 4.17 Real-time alpha flux estimation (plant signal (solid line), neural signal (dashed line), and estimation error (dotted–dashed line)).

$$+ w_{64}S(i_\beta(k)) + w_{65}S(v(k))S(\hat{x}_3(k)) + w_{66}S(v(k))S(\hat{x}_4(k))$$
$$+ w_{67}S(\hat{x}_3(k))S(\hat{x}_4(k)) + w_{68}u_\beta(k) + g_6e(k), \qquad (4.38)$$

where $S(x(k)) = \alpha \tan h(\beta x(k)) + \gamma$, $\hat{x}_1(k)$ is used to estimate $q_m(k)$, $\hat{x}_2(k)$ to estimate $v(k)$, $\hat{x}_3(k)$ to estimate $\psi_\alpha(k)$, $\hat{x}_4(k)$ to estimate $\psi_\beta(k)$, $\hat{x}_5(k)$ to estimate $i_\alpha(k)$, and $\hat{x}_6(k)$ to estimate $i_\beta(k)$. The input signals u_α and u_β are selected as chirp functions. In this application, the neural identifier is designed for x_1, x_4, and x_5, then the RONO is designed for x_2 and x_3. Both the NN and LIM states

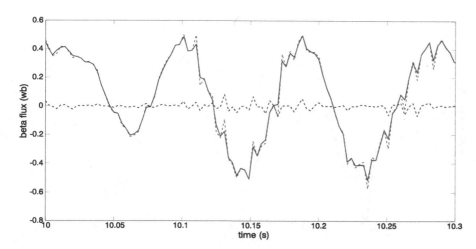

FIGURE 4.18 Real-time beta flux estimation (plant signal (solid line), neural signal (dashed line), and estimation error (dotted–dashed line)).

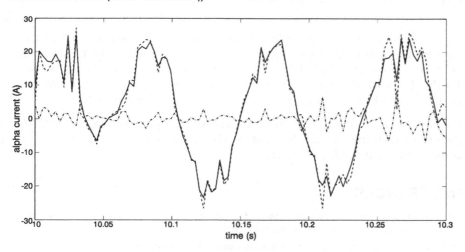

FIGURE 4.19 Real-time alpha current estimation (plant signal (solid line), neural signal (dashed line), and estimation error (dotted–dashed line)).

are initialized randomly. The associated covariance matrices are initialized as diagonals.

This RONO is implemented online on the same benchmark as described in Section 3.3.3.3. It is important to remark that the EKF used to develop the RHONN is an online learning algorithm, and is performed using a parallel configuration for fluxes and a series–parallel configuration for the measurable variables, both of them are computing between samplings.

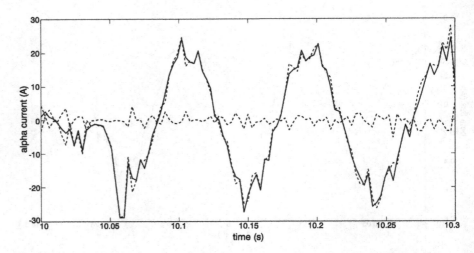

FIGURE 4.20 Real-time beta current estimation (plant signal (solid line), neural signal (dashed line), and estimation error (dotted–dashed line)).

The results of the real-time implementation are presented as follows: Fig. 4.15 displays the estimation performance for the position; Fig. 4.16 presents the velocity performance, Figs. 4.17 and 4.18 present the estimation performance for the fluxes in phase α and β, respectively. Figs. 4.19 and 4.20 portray the estimation performance for currents in phase α and β, respectively.

Finally, it is important to note that for all these examples the proposed RONO combined with the Neural Identifier builds a mathematical model for the assumed unknown nonlinear system.

REFERENCES

[1] J. Sarangapani, Neural Network Control of Nonlinear Discrete-Time Systems, CRC Press, Taylor & Francis Group, Boca Raton, FL, USA, 2006.

[2] Y.H. Kim, F.L. Lewis, High-Level Feedback Control with Neural Networks, World Scientific, Singapore, 1998.

[3] A.S. Poznyak, E.N. Sanchez, W. Yu, Differential Neural Networks for Robust Nonlinear Control, World Scientific, Singapore, 2001.

[4] A.G. Loukianov, J. Rivera, J.M. Cañedo, Discrete-time sliding mode control of an induction motor, in: Proceedings IFAC'02, Barcelona, Spain, July 2002.

[5] Q. Zhu, L. Guo, Stable adaptive neurocontrol for nonlinear discrete-time systems, IEEE Transactions on Neural Networks 15 (3) (May 2004) 653–662.

[6] V. Utkin, J. Guldner, J. Shi, Sliding Mode Control in Electromechanical Systems, Taylor and Francis, Philadelphia, USA, 1999.

[7] A.Y. Alanis, E.N. Sanchez, L.J. Ricalde, Discrete-time reduced order neural observers for uncertain nonlinear systems, International Journal of Neural Systems 20 (1) (February 2010) 29–38.

[8] A.Y. Alanis, M. Hernandez-Gonzalez, E.A. Hernandez-Vargas, Observers for biological systems, Applied Soft Computing 24 (2014) 1175–1182.

[9] A.Y. Alanis, M. Lopez-Franco, N. Arana-Daniel, C. Lopez-Franco, Discrete-time neural control for electrically driven nonholonomic mobile robots, International Journal of Adaptive Control and Signal Processing 26 (7) (June 2012) 630–644.

[10] G.A. Rovithakis, M.A. Chistodoulou, Adaptive Control with Recurrent High-Order Neural Networks, Springer-Verlag, New York, USA, 2000.

[11] Y.H. Kim, F.L. Lewis, High-Level Feedback Control with Neural Networks, World Scientific, Singapore, 1998.

[12] A.U. Levin, K.S. Narendra, Control of nonlinear dynamical systems using neural networks – part II: observability, identification and control, IEEE Transactions on Neural Networks 7 (1) (January 1996) 30–42.

[13] R. Marino, Observers for single output nonlinear systems, IEEE Transactions on Automatic Control 35 (September 1990) 1054–1058.

[14] A.N. Lakhal, A.S. Tlili, N. Benhadj Braiek, Neural network observer for nonlinear systems application to induction motors, International Journal of Control and Automation 3 (1) (2010) 1–16.

[15] I. Salgado, I. Chairez, Nonlinear discrete time neural network observer, Neurocomputing 101 (2013) 73–81.

[16] I. Chairez, Differential neural network observer, IEEE Transactions on Neural Networks 20 (9) (2009).

[17] A.N. Lakhal, A. Tlili, Comparative analysis between multimodel and neural state observation approach of nonlinear systems. Application to induction motors, vol. 1, in: Proceedings Engineering and Technology, 2013.

[18] M. Van, H.-J. Kang, Y.-S. Suh, A novel neural second-order sliding mode observer for robust fault diagnosis in robot manipulators, International Journal of Precision Engineering and Manufacturing 14 (3) (2013) 397–406.

[19] Y. Li, S. Tong, T. Li, Lecture Notes in Computer Science, Springer, Heidelberg, 2013, pp. 260–267.

[20] J. Liu, Adaptive RBF observer design and sliding mode control, in: Radial Basis Function (RBF) Neural Network Control for Mechanical Systems, Springer, Heidelberg, 2013, pp. 339–362.

[21] H.A. Talebi, F. Abdollahi, R.V. Patel, K. Khorasani, Neural Network-Based State Estimation of Nonlinear Systems, Lecture Notes in Control and Information Sciences, vol. 395, Springer, Heidelberg, 2010.

[22] J. Na, G. Herrmann, X. Ren, P. Barber, Adaptive discrete neural observer design for nonlinear systems with unknown time-delay, International Journal of Robust and Nonlinear Control 21 (2011) 625–647.

[23] A.Y. Alanis, E.N. Sanchez, A.G. Loukianov, M. Perez, Real-time recurrent neural state estimation, IEEE Transactions on Neural Networks 22 (3) (2011) 497–505.

[24] E.A. Hernandez-Vargas, E.N. Sanchez, J.F. Beteau, C. Cadet, Neural observer based hybrid intelligent scheme for activated sludge wastewater treatment, Chemical and Biochemical Engineering Quarterly 23 (3) (2009) 377–384.

[25] E.A. Hernandez-Vargas, A.Y. Alanis, E.N. Sanchez, Discrete-time neural observer for HIV infection dynamics, in: World Automation Congress Proceedings, 2012, Art. No. 6320891.

[26] A. Johanssona, A. Medvedeva, An observer for systems with nonlinear output map, Automatica 39 (2003) 09.

[27] S. Oh, H. Khallil, Nonlinear output-feedback tracking using high-gain observer and variable structure control, Automatica 33 (10) (1997) 1845–1856.

CHAPTER 5

Neural Observers with Unknown Time-Delays

ABSTRACT

This chapter deals with the extension of the full and reduced order neural observers, respectively, for discrete-time nonlinear systems under the presence of unknown time delays. The designed observers are applied to a van der Pol system and to electromechanical systems.

KEYWORDS

Full order observers

Reduced order observers

Neural observers

Unknown discrete-time nonlinear delayed systems

Rotatory induction motors

Linear induction motors

van der Pol system

CONTENTS

5.1 INTRODUCTION

Analysis of time-delay systems has become an important field of research due to its frequent presence in engineering applications [1,2,5,6], as in chemical processes, engine cooling systems, hydraulic systems, irrigation channels, metallurgical processing systems, network control systems, and supply networks, among others [1,5,6].

Delays in systems are caused by the limited capabilities of their components to process data and also by transporting information and materials [3]. Therefore, the main sources of time delay are [4]:

- *Nature of the process* which arises when the system has to wait a certain time in order to continue to the next step; for example, this happens in chemical reactors, diesel engines, and recycling processes.
- *Transport delay* which occurs when systems must transport materials and the controller takes time to affect the process; for example, in rolling mills, cooling, and heating systems.

Discrete-Time Neural Observers. DOI:10.1016/B978-0-12-810543-6.00005-8

- *Communication delay* can occur due to:
  - *Propagation time delay* of signals among actuators, controllers, sensors, especially in networking control and fault-tolerant systems.
  - *Access time delay* as a result of a finite time required to access a shared media. The data at the controller are a delayed version of the current state, and the control action suffers from a time delay when it is sent. Such a situation is found in network systems.

Delays can be constant or time-varying, known or unknown, deterministic or stochastic, depending on the system under consideration [3]. It is well-known that delays could induce instability and poor performance. A number of methodologies have been proposed to handle these problems [2,5,7,8,6], some of them based on Neural Networks used to deal with unknown dynamics [2,7,9–11]. Most of them are developed for continuous-time systems. Moreover, loss of packets in network systems can happen as a result of delays which are introduced due to the limited capacity of data transmission between devices [12], which can also result in instability [10,11].

In order to control a system, a model is usually required, which is mathematical structure knowledge about the system represented in the form of differential or difference equations. The development of mathematical descriptions for dynamical systems is motivated by simulation, prediction, fault detection, and control system design, among others [13].

There are two ways to obtain a system model: it can be derived in a deductive manner using the laws of physics, or it can be inferred from a set of data collected during experiments through its operating range [13]. The first method can be simple; however, in many cases the required time for getting the model can be excessive; moreover, obtaining an accurate model this way would be unrealistic because of unknown dynamics and delays that cannot be modeled. The second method, which is known as system identification, could be a helpful shortcut for deriving the model. Despite the fact that system identification does not always result in an accurate model, a satisfactory one can be obtained with reasonable efforts [13].

There are many methods to accomplish system identification; just to name a few, we mention those based on neural networks, fuzzy logic, auxiliary model identification, and hierarchical identification [14]. Neural networks stand out for their characteristics, such as no need to establish the system model structure; any linear and nonlinear model can be identified. Neural networks allow identifying and obtaining mathematical models which are close to the actual system behaviors even in the presence of variations and disturbances [14,13].

Recurrent Neural Networks (RNNs) are a special kind of Neural Network with feedback connections, which have an impact on the learning capabilities and performance; moreover, unit-delay elements on the feedback loops result in a nonlinear dynamical behavior [15].

Recurrent High Order Neural Networks (RHONNs) are an extension of the first order Hopfield network. A Recurrent High Order Neural Network has more interaction among its neurons and characteristics, including approximation capabilities, easy implementation, robustness against noise and online training, which make it ideal for modeling complex nonlinear systems [16].

Backpropagation through time learning is the most used training algorithm for RNNs; however, it is a first order gradient descent method. So even if it gives good results on several occasions, it presents problems such as slow convergence, high complexity, bifurcations, instability, and limited applicability due to high computational costs [17,16], and it is not able to discover contingencies spanning long temporal intervals due to the vanishing gradient [18, 19]. On the other hand, training algorithms which are based on the Extended Kalman Filter (EKF) improve learning convergence, reduce the epoch number and the number of required neurons. Moreover, EKF training methods for training feedforward and recurrent Neural Networks have proven to be reliable and practical [20,16].

In this chapter, an RHONN trained with an EKF based algorithm is used to develop neural observers for discrete-time nonlinear deterministic MIMO systems with unknown time delays, first with the full-order approach and then with the reduced-order one. In order to prove that the RHONN observer trained with an EKF based algorithm is Semi-Globally Uniformly Ultimately Bounded (SGUUB), a Lyapunov stability analysis is included for both cases. Finally, two applications are considered for the proposed observers.

A number of methodologies have been proposed for designing observers for non-linear time-delay systems [7,21–27]. These observers need knowledge about the plant and at least an approximation of the time-delay; moreover, most of them are designed for the continuous-time case, and just a few work with neural networks to deal with unknown dynamics [7,26,27].

In this chapter, an RHONN observer trained with an EKF based algorithm for discrete-time nonlinear deterministic MIMO systems with unknown time delay is proposed with the following advantages:

- This RHONN observer does not require previous knowledge of the system model.
- For this RHONN observer, knowledge about the delay, its estimation or its bounds is not necessary.
- For this RHONN observer, measurements, estimates or bounds of disturbances are not necessary.
- The mentioned characteristics of the proposed RHONN observer make it ideal for digital devices which require real-time implementation.

5.2 TIME-DELAY NONLINEAR SYSTEM

Time-delay is the property of physical systems by which the response to an applied unit, as well as its effects, is delayed [29]. Whenever material, information or energy is transmitted, there is an associated delay, and its value is determined by the distance and speed of the transmission [29].

Time-Delay Systems (TDSs), also known as systems with after effect or dead-time, hereditary systems, equations with deviating argument or differential-difference equations, are systems which have a significant time-delay between the application of the inputs and their effects. TDSs inherit time-delay in their components or from introduction of delays for control design purposes [28, 30,31].

In general, TDSs can be classified as [3]:

- Systems with lumped delays where a finite number of parameters can describe their delay phenomena.
- Systems with distributed delays where it is not possible to find a finite number of parameters which describe their time delay phenomena.

The presence of delays in such systems makes system analysis and control design complex and also can degrade the performance or induce instability [28, 29]. This is the reason for the importance of understanding delays in systems, otherwise, they could become unstable [29].

Consider the following discrete time-delay nonlinear MIMO system described by

$$x(k+1) = F(x(k-l), u(k)), \qquad (5.1)$$
$$y(k) = h(x(k)), \qquad (5.2)$$

where $x \in \mathfrak{R}^n$ is the state vector of the system, $u \in \mathfrak{R}^m$ is the input vector, $y \in \mathfrak{R}^p$ is the output vector, $C \in \mathfrak{R}^{p \times n}$ is a known output matrix, $d \in \mathfrak{R}^n$ is a disturbance vector, $F \in \mathfrak{R}^n \times \mathfrak{R}^m \to \mathfrak{R}^n$ is a nonlinear function, and $l = 1, 2, \ldots$ is the unknown delay.

The system (5.1)–(5.2) can be rewritten as

$$x(k-l) = [x_i(k-l) \ldots x_i(k-l) \ldots x_n(k-l)]^\top,$$
$$d(k) = [d_i(k) \ldots d_i(k) \ldots d_n(k)]^\top,$$
$$x_i(k+1) = F_i(x(k-l), u(k)) + d_i(k),$$
$$y(x) = Cx(k),$$
$$i = 1, 2, \ldots, n. \qquad (5.3)$$

5.3 FULL ORDER NEURAL OBSERVERS FOR UNKNOWN NONLINEAR SYSTEMS WITH DELAYS

For system (5.3), the following recurrent high order neural observer structure is proposed:

$$\widehat{x}(k) = [\widehat{x}_1(k) \ldots \widehat{x}_i(k) \ldots \widehat{x}_n(k)]^\top,$$
$$\widehat{x}_i(k+1) = w_i^T z_i(\widehat{x}(k), u(k)) + g_i e(k),$$
$$\widehat{y}(k) = C\widehat{x}(k),$$
$$i = 1, 2, \ldots, n, \tag{5.4}$$

where $\widehat{x}_i$ $(i = 1, 2, \ldots, n)$ is the state of the ith neuron, w_i is the respective online adapted weight vector, n is the state dimension, and $z_i(\bullet)$ is given by

$$z_i(\widehat{x}_i(k), u(k)) = \begin{bmatrix} z_{i_1} \\ z_{i_2} \\ \vdots \\ z_{i_{L_i}} \end{bmatrix} = \begin{bmatrix} \Pi_{j \in I_1} \xi_{ij}^{d_{ij}(1)} \\ \Pi_{j \in I_2} \xi_{ij}^{d_{ij}(2)} \\ \vdots \\ \Pi_{j \in I_{L_i}} \xi_{ij}^{d_{ij}(L_i)} \end{bmatrix} \tag{5.5}$$

with L_i as the respective number of high-order connections, $\{I_1, I_2, \ldots, I_{L_i}\}$ a collection of unordered subsets of $\{1, 2, \ldots, n+m\}$, m the number of external inputs, $d_{ij}(k)$ being non-negative integers, and ξ_i defined as follows:

$$\xi_i = \begin{bmatrix} \xi_{i_1} \\ \vdots \\ \xi_{i_n} \\ \xi_{i_{n+1}} \\ \vdots \\ \xi_{i_{n+m}} \end{bmatrix} = \begin{bmatrix} S(x_1(k-l)) \\ \vdots \\ S(x_n(k-l)) \\ u_1(k) \\ \vdots \\ u_m(k) \end{bmatrix}. \tag{5.6}$$

In (5.6), $u = [u_1, u_2, \ldots, u_m]^\top$ is the input vector to the Neural Network, and $S(\bullet)$ is defined by

$$S(\varsigma) = \frac{1}{1 + \exp(-\beta\varsigma)} \tag{5.7}$$

where $\beta > 0$ and ς is any real-valued variable. Define w^* as the ideal weights vector and let w_i be its estimate. Then the weights estimation error and the state estimation error are defined as:

$$\tilde{w}_i(k) = w_i^* - w_i(k), \tag{5.8}$$
$$\tilde{x}_i(k) = x_i(k) - \widehat{x}_i(k). \tag{5.9}$$

Given the dynamics of (5.9), system (5.3) can be approximated by the following RHONN [32]:

$$x_i(k+1) = w_i^{*T} z_i(x(k-l), u(k)) + \epsilon_{z_i}, \tag{5.10}$$

therefore

$$\tilde{x}_i(k+1) = x_i(k+1) - \widehat{x}_i(k+1),$$
$$\tilde{x}_i(k+1) = w_i^{*T} z_i(x(k-l), u(k)) + \epsilon_{z_i}$$
$$- w_i^T z_i(\widehat{x}(k), u(k)) - g_i e(k). \tag{5.11}$$

Adding and subtracting $w_i^{*T} z_i(\widehat{x}_i(k), u(k))$, we get

$$\tilde{x}_i(k+1) = \tilde{w}_i^T(k) z_i(\widehat{x}_i(k), u(k)) + \epsilon'_{z_i} - g_i e(k) \tag{5.12}$$

with

$$\epsilon'_{z_i} = w_i^{*T} z_i(\tilde{x}(k), u(k)) + \epsilon_{z_i},$$
$$z_i(\tilde{x}(k), u(k)) = z_i(x(k-l), u(k)) - z_i(\widehat{x}(k), u(k)).$$

5.3.1 Extended Kalman Filter Training Algorithm

The EKF-based training algorithm, used for getting the weights vector for the RHONN observer in this chapter, is

$$w_i(k+1) = w_i(k) + \eta_i K_i(k) e(k), \tag{5.13}$$
$$K_i(k) = P_i(k) H_i(k) M_i(k),$$
$$P_i(k+1) = P_i(k) - K_i(k) H_i^\top(k) P_i(k) + Q_i(k),$$

with $i = 1, \ldots, n$ and

$$M_i(k) = \left[R_i(k) + H_i^\top(k) P_i(k) H_i(k) \right]^{-1}, \tag{5.14}$$

$$H_{ij} = \left[\frac{\partial \widehat{x}_i(k)}{\partial w_{ij}(k)} \right]^T, \tag{5.15}$$

and the output error is

$$e(k) = y_i(k) - \widehat{y}_i(k),$$
$$e(k) = C\tilde{x}(k), \tag{5.16}$$

where $e_i \in \Re^p$ is the output error, $P_i \in \Re^{L_i \times L_i}$ is the weight estimation error covariance matrix, $w_i \in \Re^{L_i}$ is the online adapted weight vector, $K_i \in \Re^{L_i}$ is the Kalman gain vector, $Q_i \in \Re^{L_i \times L_i}$ is the estimation noise covariance matrix, $R_i \in \Re$ is the error noise covariance matrix, $H_i \in \Re^{L_i}$ is a vector in which each entry H_{ij} is the derivative of the Neural Network state $(\widehat{x}_i)$ with respect to the Neural Network weight (w_{ij}) and it is given by (5.15), where $i = 1, \ldots, n$ and $j = 1, \ldots, L_i$. P_i and Q_i are initialized as diagonal matrices with entries $P_i(0)$ and $Q_i(0)$, respectively. It is important to remark that $H_i(k)$, $K_i(k)$, and $P_i(k)$ for the EKF are bounded [33].

Considering (5.13) and the fact that w^* is constant, the dynamics of (5.8) is

$$\tilde{w}_i(k+1) - \tilde{w}_i(k) = w_i(k+1) - w_i(k),$$
$$\tilde{w}_i(k+1) = \tilde{w}_i(k) - \eta_i K_i(k) e_i(k). \tag{5.17}$$

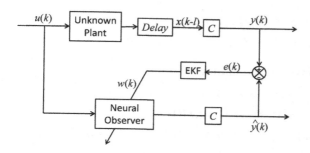

FIGURE 5.1 Full order neural observer scheme for nonlinear systems with delays.

The proposed neural observer scheme is shown in Fig. 5.1.

Considering (5.3)–(5.17), we establish the first main result of this chapter as the following theorem.

Theorem 5.1. *For system (5.3), the RHONN (5.4) trained with the EKF-based algorithm (5.13), ensures that the estimation error (5.9) and the output error (5.16) are Semi-Globally Uniformly Ultimately Bounded (SGUUB); moreover, the RHONN weights remain bounded.*

Proof. Consider the candidate Lyapunov function

$$V_i(k) = \widetilde{w}_i^T(k)\, P_i(k)\, \widetilde{w}_i(k) + \widetilde{x}_i^T(k)\, \widetilde{x}_i(k) \tag{5.18}$$

whose first increment is defined as

$$
\begin{aligned}
\Delta V_i(k) &= V_i(k+1) - V_i(k) \\
&= \widetilde{w}_i^T(k+1)\, P_i(k+1)\, \widetilde{w}_i(k+1) + \widetilde{x}_i^T(k+1)\, \widetilde{x}_i(k+1) \\
&\quad - \widetilde{w}_i^T(k)\, P_i(k)\, \widetilde{w}_i(k) - \widetilde{x}_i^T(k)\, \widetilde{x}_i(k).
\end{aligned}
\tag{5.19}
$$

Substituting (5.12), (5.13), and (5.17) into (5.19) yields

$$
\begin{aligned}
\Delta V_i(k) &= \big[\widetilde{w}_i(k) - \eta_i K_i(k) C\widetilde{x}(k)\big]^T [A_i(k)]\big[\widetilde{w}_i(k) - \eta_i K_i(k) C\widetilde{x}(k)\big] \\
&\quad + \big[f(k) - g_i C\widetilde{x}(k)\big]^T \big[f(k) - g_i C\widetilde{x}(k)\big] \\
&\quad - \widetilde{w}_i^T(k)\, P_i(k)\, \widetilde{w}_i(k) - \widetilde{x}_i^T(k)\, \widetilde{x}_i(k) \\
&= -\widetilde{w}_i^T(k)\, B_i(k)\, \widetilde{w}_i(k) - \eta_i \widetilde{x}^T(k)\, C^T K_i^T(k)\, A_i(k)\, \widetilde{w}_i(k) \\
&\quad - \eta_i \widetilde{w}_i^T(k)\, A_i(k)\, C\widetilde{x}(k) + \eta_i^2 \widetilde{x}^T(k)\, C^T K_i^T(k)\, A_i(k)\, K_i(k)\, C\widetilde{x}(k) \\
&\quad + f^T(k)\, f(k) - f^T(k)\, g_i C\widetilde{x}(k) - \widetilde{x}^T(k)\, C^T g_i^T f(k) \\
&\quad + \widetilde{x}^T(k)\, C^T g_i^T g_i C\widetilde{x}(k) - \widetilde{x}_i^T(k)\, \widetilde{x}_i(k)
\end{aligned}
\tag{5.20}
$$

with

$$A_i(k) = P_i(k) - B(k),$$

$$B(k) = K_i(k) H_i^T(k) P_i(k) + Q_i(k),$$
$$f(k) = \widetilde{w}_i^T(k) z_i(\widehat{x}(k-l), u(k)) + \epsilon'_{z_i}.$$

Using the following inequalities:

$$X^T X + Y^T Y \geq -X^T Y - Y^T X,$$
$$-\lambda_{\min}(P) X^2 \geq -X^T P X \geq -\lambda_{\max}(P) X^2,$$

which are valid $\forall X, Y \in \Re^n$, $\forall P \in \Re^{n \times n}$, $P = P^T > 0$, expression (5.20) can be rewritten as

$$\begin{aligned}
\Delta V_i(k) \leq &-\|\widetilde{w}_i(k)\|^2 \lambda_{\min}(B_i(k)) + 2\|f(k)\|^2 \\
&+ \eta_i^2 \|\widetilde{x}(k)\|^2 \|C\|^2 \|K_i(k)\|^2 \lambda_{\max} A_i(k) \\
&+ 2\|\widetilde{x}(k)\|^2 \|C\|^2 \|g_i\|^2 - \|\widetilde{x}(k)\|^2 \\
&+ \|K_i(k)\|^2 \|A_i(k)\|^2 \|\widetilde{w}_i(k)\|^2 + \eta_i^2 \|\widetilde{x}(k)\|^2 \|C\|^2.
\end{aligned} \tag{5.21}$$

Replacing $f(k)$ in (5.21), we obtain

$$\begin{aligned}
\Delta V_i(k) \leq &-\|\widetilde{w}_i(k)\|^2 \lambda_{\min}(B_i(k)) + 2\|\widetilde{w}_i(k)\|^2 \|z_i(\widehat{x}(k-l), u(k))\|^2 \\
&+ \eta_i^2 \|\widetilde{x}(k)\|^2 \|C\|^2 \|K_i(k)\|^2 \lambda_{\max} A_i(k) \\
&+ 2\|\widetilde{x}(k)\|^2 \|C\|^2 \|g_i\|^2 - \|\widetilde{x}(k)\|^2 + \eta_i^2 \|\widetilde{x}(k)\|^2 \|C\|^2 \\
&+ \|K_i(k)\|^2 \|A_i(k)\|^2 \|\widetilde{w}_i(k)\|^2 + 2|\epsilon'_{z_i}|^2.
\end{aligned} \tag{5.22}$$

Defining

$$E_i(k) = \lambda_{\min}(B_i(k)) - \|K_i(k)\|^2 \|A_i(k)\|^2 - 2\|z_i(\widehat{x}(k-l), u(k))\|^2, \tag{5.23}$$
$$F_i(k) = 1 - \eta_i^2 \|C\|^2 \|K_i(k)\|^2 \lambda_{\max} A_i(k) - 2\|C\|^2 \|g_i\|^2 - \eta_i^2 \|C\|^2, \tag{5.24}$$

inequality (5.22) can be expressed as

$$\Delta V_i(k) \leq -\|\widetilde{w}_i(k)\|^2 E_i(k) - \|\widetilde{x}(k)\|^2 F_i(k) + 2|\epsilon'_{z_i}|^2.$$

Hence, $\Delta V_i(k) < 0$, whenever

$$\|\widetilde{x}(k)\|^2 > \sqrt{\frac{2|\epsilon'_{z_i}|^2}{F_i(k)}}$$

or

$$\|\widetilde{w}_i(k)\|^2 > \sqrt{\frac{2|\epsilon'_{z_i}|^2}{E_i(k)}}.$$

Therefore, the solution of (5.11) and (5.17) is stable; hence the estimation error and the RHONN weights are SGUUB. Now, to proceed with the proof, consider a Lyapunov function candidate

$$V_i(k) = \sum_{i=1}^{n} (\widetilde{w}_i(k) P_i(k) \widetilde{w}_i(k) + \widetilde{x}_i(k) \widetilde{x}_i(k)) \tag{5.25}$$

whose first increment is defined as

$$\Delta V_i (k) = \sum_{i=1}^{n} (\widetilde{w}_i (k+1) P_i (k+1) \widetilde{w}_i (k+1)$$
$$+ \widetilde{x}_i (k+1) \widetilde{x}_i (k+1)$$
$$- \widetilde{w}_i (k) P_i (k) \widetilde{w}_i (k)$$
$$- \widetilde{x}_i (k) P_i (k) \widetilde{x}_i (k)) . \tag{5.26}$$

Therefore, as above, (5.26) can be expressed as

$$\Delta V_i (k) \leq \sum_{i=1}^{n} \left(-\|\widetilde{w}_i (k)\|^2 E_i (k) - \|\widetilde{x} (k)\|^2 F_i (k) + 2 \left| \epsilon'_{z_i} \right|^2 \right)$$

with $E_i (k)$ and $F_i (k)$ as in (5.23) and (5.24), respectively. As a result, $\Delta V_i (k) < 0$ whenever

$$\|\widetilde{x} (k)\| > \kappa_1 (k)$$

or

$$\|\widetilde{w}_i (k)\| > \kappa_2 (k) ,$$

and if $\|\widetilde{x} (k)\| > \kappa_1 (k)$ and $\|\widetilde{w}_i (k)\| > \kappa_2 (k)$, $\forall i = 1, \ldots, n$ holds, then $\Delta V_i (k) < 0$. Finally, considering (5.8) and (5.9), it is easy to see that the output error has an algebraic relation with $\widetilde{x} (k)$. For this reason, if $\widetilde{x} (k)$ is bounded, $e (k)$ is bounded, too:

$$e (k) = y (k) - \widehat{y} (k) = Cx (k) - C\widehat{x} (k) = C\widetilde{x} (k) ,$$
$$\|e (k)\| = \|C\| \|\widetilde{x} (k)\| . \qquad \square$$

Considering Theorem 5.1 and its proof, it can be easily shown that the result can be extended to systems with multiple delays like $x (k - l_i)$ with $i = 1, 2, \ldots,$ instead of $x (k - l)$ in (5.3) and/or for time-varying delays $x (k - l_i (k))$ with bounded $l_i (k)$ bounded by l, i.e., $l_i (k) \leq l$.

5.4 REDUCED ORDER NEURAL OBSERVERS FOR UNKNOWN NONLINEAR SYSTEMS WITH DELAYS

As in Chapter 4, in order to reduce the computational complexity, in this section we propose the use of a reduced order neural observer, which uses the available measurement and estimates only the unmeasurable variables; furthermore, the proposed observer provides mathematical models for unknown nonlinear systems with delays. Finally, it is important to note that for all these examples, the proposed RONO combined with the Neural Identifier builds a mathematical model for the assumed unknown nonlinear system.

For system (4.6), we propose a reduced order neural observer (RONO) with the following structure:

$$\widehat{x}(k) = \left[\ \widehat{x}_1(k)\ \ \dots\ \ \widehat{x}_n(k)\ \right]^{\top},$$
$$\widehat{x}_i(k+1) = w_i^{\top} z_i(x_a(k-l), \widehat{x}_b(k)u(k)) + g_i e(k),$$
$$\widehat{x}_j(k+1) = w_j^{\top} z_j(x_a(k-l), u(k)) + g_j e(k), \tag{5.27}$$
$$\widehat{y}(k) = C\widehat{x}(k)$$

with

$$x_a(k-l) = \left[\ x_1(k-l)\ \ \dots\ \ x_i(k-l)\ \ \dots\ \ x_p(k-l)\ \right],$$
$$\widehat{x}_b(k) = \left[\ \widehat{x}_{p+1}(k)\ \ \dots\ \ \widehat{x}_j(k)\ \ \dots\ \ \widehat{x}_n(k)\ \right]$$

and $i = 1, \dots, p$, $j = p+1, \dots, n$, g_i, $g_j \in \Re^p$, w_i, w_j, z_i, and z_j as in (2.7). As explained in Chapter 4, $f_a(\bullet)$ and $f_b(\bullet)$ are unknown nonlinear functions, for which x_a are the measurable variables and x_b are the unmeasurable variables. Hence, in this section, we consider a neural identifier for x_a and a neural observer to estimate x_b for system (4.6), which is assumed to be observable. The weight vectors are updated online with a decoupled EKF (5.13), the output error is defined by

$$e(k) = y(k) - \widehat{y}(k) \tag{5.28}$$

and the state estimation error is

$$\widetilde{x}(k) = x(k) - \widehat{x}(k). \tag{5.29}$$

Considering (5.28) and (5.29) gives

$$e(k) = C\widetilde{x}(k). \tag{5.30}$$

Hence, the dynamics of $x_i(k+1)$ can be expressed as

$$\widetilde{x}_i(k+1) = x_i(k+1) - \widehat{x}_i(k+1). \tag{5.31}$$

Then

$$\widetilde{x}_i(k+1) = w_i^{*\top} z_i(x(k-l), u(k)) + \epsilon_{z_i}$$
$$- w_i^{\top}(k) z_i(x_a(k-l), \widehat{x}_b(k), u(k)) - g_i e(k). \tag{5.32}$$

Adding and subtracting $w_i^{*\top} z_i(x_a(k-l), \widehat{x}_b(k)u(k))$, expression (5.32) can be written as

$$\widetilde{x}_i(k+1) = \widetilde{w}_i^{\top}(k) z_i(x_a(k-l), \widehat{x}_b(k), u(k)) + \epsilon_{z_i}' - g_i e(k) \tag{5.33}$$

with

$$\epsilon_{z_i}' = w_i^{*\top} z_i(\widetilde{x}(k-l), u(k)) + \epsilon_{z_i}, \tag{5.34}$$
$$z_i(\widetilde{x}(k-l), u(k)) = z_i(x(k-l), u(k)) - z_i(x_a(k-l), \widehat{x}_b(k), u(k)).$$

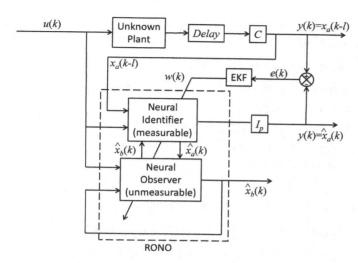

FIGURE 5.2 Reduced order neural observer scheme for nonlinear systems with delays.

It is clear from (5.34) that ϵ'_{z_i} is a bounded since ϵ_{z_i} and $z_i\left(\widetilde{x}(k-l), u(k)\right)$ terms are individually bounded above [34]. On the other hand, the dynamics of $x_j\,(k+1)$ can be expressed as

$$\widetilde{x}_j\,(k+1) = x_j\,(k+1) - \widehat{x}_j\,(k+1), \tag{5.35}$$

$$\widetilde{x}_j\,(k+1) = \widetilde{w}_j^{\top}\,(k)\,z_j(x_a(k-l), u(k)) + \epsilon'_{z_j} - g_j e\,(k) \tag{5.36}$$

with

$$\epsilon'_{z_j} = w_j^{*\top} z_j\left(\widetilde{x}(k-l), u(k)\right) + \epsilon_{z_j}, \tag{5.37}$$

$$z_j\left(\widetilde{x}(k-l), u(k)\right) = z_j\left(x(k-l), u(k)\right) - z_j(x_a(k-l), u(k)).$$

It is clear from (5.37) that ϵ'_{z_j} is bounded since ϵ_{z_j} and $z_j\left(\widetilde{x}(k-l), u(k)\right)$ terms are individually bounded above [34]. Besides the dynamics of (5.8) is

$$\widetilde{w}_i\,(k+1) = \widetilde{w}_i\,(k) - \eta_i K_i\,(k)\,e\,(k), \quad i = 1, 2, \ldots, n. \tag{5.38}$$

The proposed reduced order neural observer scheme is shown in Fig. 5.2.

Considering (5.27)–(5.38), we establish the second main result of this chapter as the following theorem.

Theorem 5.2. *For system (5.3), the RONO (5.27), trained with the EKF-based algorithm (5.13), ensures that the estimation error (5.29) and the output error (5.30) are semi-globally uniformly ultimately bounded (SGUUB); moreover, the RONO weights remain bounded.*

Proof. We consider the component-wise form of a Lyapunov function candidate in two cases.

Case 1. Measurable variables. For x_i with $i = 1, \ldots, p$, consider the Lyapunov function candidate

$$V_i(k) = \widetilde{w}_i(k) P_i(k) \widetilde{w}_i(k) + \widetilde{x}_i(k) \widetilde{x}_i(k) \tag{5.39}$$

whose first increment is defined as

$$\begin{aligned}
\Delta V_i(k) &= V(k+1) - V(k) \\
&= \widetilde{w}_i(k+1) P_i(k+1) \widetilde{w}_i(k+1) \\
&\quad + \widetilde{x}_i(k+1) \widetilde{x}_i(k+1) \\
&\quad - \widetilde{w}_i(k) P_i(k) \widetilde{w}_i(k) \\
&\quad - \widetilde{x}_i(k) \widetilde{x}_i(k).
\end{aligned} \tag{5.40}$$

Using (5.13), (5.33), and (5.38) in (5.40) yields

$$\begin{aligned}
\Delta V_i(k) &= \left[\widetilde{w}_i(k) - \eta_i K_i(k) e(k) \right]^T [A_i(k)] \left[\widetilde{w}_i(k) - \eta_i K_i(k) e(k) \right] \\
&\quad + \left[f(k) - g_i C \widetilde{x}(k) \right]^T [A_i(k)] \left[f(k) - g_i C \widetilde{x}(k) \right] \\
&\quad - \widetilde{w}_i(k) P_i(k) \widetilde{w}_i(k) - \widetilde{x}_i(k) P_i(k) \widetilde{x}_i(k) \\
&= -\widetilde{w}_i^T(k) B_i(k) \widetilde{w}_i(k) - \eta_i \widetilde{x}^T(k) C^T K_i^T(k) A_i(k) \widetilde{w}_i(k) \\
&\quad - \eta_i \widetilde{w}_i^T(k) A_i(k) C \widetilde{x}(k) + \eta_i^2 \widetilde{x}^T(k) C^T K_i^T(k) A_i(k) K_i(k) C \widetilde{x}(k) \\
&\quad + f^T(k) f(k) - f^T(k) g_i C \widetilde{x}(k) - \widetilde{x}^T(k) C^T g_i^T f(k) \\
&\quad + \widetilde{x}^T(k) C^T g_i^T g_i C \widetilde{x}(k) - \widetilde{x}_i^T(k) \widetilde{x}_i(k)
\end{aligned} \tag{5.41}$$

with

$$A_i(k) = P_i(k) - B_i(k),$$
$$B_i(k) = K_i(k) H_i^\top(k) P_i(k) + Q_i(k),$$
$$f_i(k) = \widetilde{w}_i(k) z_i(x_a(k), \widehat{x}_b(k), u(k)) + \epsilon'_{z_i}.$$

Using the following inequalities:

$$X^T X + Y^T Y \geq -X^T Y - Y^T X,$$
$$-\lambda_{\min}(P) X^2 \geq -X^T P X \geq -\lambda_{\max}(P) X^2,$$

which are valid $\forall X, Y \in \Re^n, \forall P \in \Re^{n \times n}, P = P^T > 0$, increment (5.41) can be bounded as follows:

$$\begin{aligned}
\Delta V_i(k) &\leq -\|\widetilde{w}_i(k)\|^2 \lambda_{\min}(B_i(k)) + 2\|f_i(k)\|^2 \\
&\quad + \eta_i^2 \|\widetilde{x}(k)\|^2 \|C\|^2 \|K_i(k)\|^2 \lambda_{\max} A_i(k) \\
&\quad + 2\|\widetilde{x}(k)\|^2 \|C\|^2 \|g_i\|^2 - \|\widetilde{x}(k)\|^2 \\
&\quad + \|K_i(k)\|^2 \|A_i(k)\|^2 \|\widetilde{w}_i(k)\|^2 + \eta_i^2 \|\widetilde{x}(k)\|^2 \|C\|^2.
\end{aligned} \tag{5.42}$$

Substituting $f_i(k) = \widetilde{w}_i(k) z_i(x_a(k-l), \widehat{x}_b(k), u(k)) + \epsilon'_{z_i}$ in (5.42) gives

$$\begin{aligned}
\Delta V_i(k) &\leq -\|\widetilde{w}_i(k)\|^2 \lambda_{\min}(B_i(k)) + 2\|\widetilde{w}_i(k)\|^2 \|z_i(x_a(k-l), \widehat{x}_b(k), u(k))\|^2 \\
&\quad + \eta_i^2 \|\widetilde{x}(k)\|^2 \|C\|^2 \|K_i(k)\|^2 \lambda_{\max} A_i(k)
\end{aligned}$$

$$+ 2 \|\widetilde{x}(k)\|^2 \|C\|^2 \|g_i\|^2 - \|\widetilde{x}(k)\|^2 + \eta_i^2 \|\widetilde{x}(k)\|^2 \|C\|^2$$
$$+ \|K_i(k)\|^2 \|A_i(k)\|^2 \|\widetilde{w}_i(k)\|^2 + 2 |\epsilon'_{z_i}|^2. \tag{5.43}$$

Defining

$$E_i(k) = \lambda_{\min}(B_i(k)) - \|K_i(k)\|^2 \|A_i(k)\|^2 - 2 \|z_i(x_a(k-l), \widehat{x}_b(k), u(k))\|^2, \tag{5.44}$$

$$F_i(k) = 1 - \eta_i^2 \|C\|^2 \|K_i(k)\|^2 \lambda_{\max} A_i(k) - 2 \|C\|^2 \|g_i\|^2 - \eta_i^2 \|C\|^2, \tag{5.45}$$

inequality (5.43) can be rewritten as

$$\Delta V_i(k) \leq -\|\widetilde{w}_i(k)\|^2 E_i(k) - \|\widetilde{x}(k)\|^2 F_i(k) + 2 |\epsilon'_{z_i}|^2.$$

Hence, $\Delta V_i(k) \leq 0$ whenever

$$\|\widetilde{x}(k)\|^2 > \sqrt{\frac{2 |\epsilon'_{z_i}|^2}{F_i(k)}}$$

or

$$\|\widetilde{w}_i(k)\|^2 > \sqrt{\frac{2 |\epsilon'_{z_i}|^2}{E_i(k)}}.$$

Therefore, the solution of (5.31) and (5.38) is SGUUB, hence the estimation error and the RONO weights are SGUUB [35].

Case 2. Unmeasurable variables. For x_j with $j = p + 1, \ldots, n$, consider a Lyapunov function candidate

$$V_j(k) = \widetilde{w}_j(k) P_j(k) \widetilde{w}_j(k) + \widetilde{x}_j(k) \widetilde{x}_j(k). \tag{5.46}$$

Using (5.13), (5.35) and (5.38), its first difference can be expressed as

$$\Delta V_j(k) = -\widetilde{w}_j^T(k) B_j(k) \widetilde{w}_j(k) - \eta_j \widetilde{x}^T(k) C^T K_j^T(k) A_j(k) \widetilde{w}_j(k)$$
$$- \eta_j \widetilde{w}_j^T(k) A_j(k) C\widetilde{x}(k) + \eta_j^2 \widetilde{x}^T(k) C^T K_j^T(k) A_i(k) K_j(k) C\widetilde{x}(k)$$
$$+ f_j^T(k) f_j(k) - f_j^T(k) g_j C\widetilde{x}(k) - \widetilde{x}^T(k) C^T g_j^T f_j(k)$$
$$+ \widetilde{x}^T(k) C^T g_j^T g_j C\widetilde{x}(k) - \widetilde{x}_j^T(k) \widetilde{x}_j(k) \tag{5.47}$$

with

$$A_j(k) = P_j(k) - B_j(k),$$
$$B_j(k) = K_j(k) H_j^T(k) P_j(k) + Q_j(k),$$
$$f_j(k) = \widetilde{w}_j(k) z_j(x_a(k-l), \widehat{x}_b(k), u(k)) + \epsilon'_{z_j}.$$

As in *Case 1*,

$$\Delta V_j(k) \leq -\|\widetilde{w}_j(k)\|^2 \lambda_{\min}(B_j(k)) + 2 \|\widetilde{w}_j(k)\|^2 \|z_j(x_a(k-l), \widehat{x}_b(k), u(k))\|^2$$
$$+ \eta_j^2 \|\widetilde{x}(k)\|^2 \|C\|^2 \|K_j(k)\|^2 \lambda_{\max} A_j(k)$$

$$+ 2 \left\| \widetilde{x}(k) \right\|^2 \left\| C \right\|^2 \left\| g_j \right\|^2 - \left\| \widetilde{x}(k) \right\|^2 + \eta_j^2 \left\| \widetilde{x}(k) \right\|^2 \left\| C \right\|^2$$
$$+ \left\| K_j(k) \right\|^2 \left\| A_j(k) \right\|^2 \left\| \widetilde{w}_j(k) \right\|^2 + 2 \left| \epsilon'_{z_j} \right|^2. \tag{5.48}$$

Defining

$$E_j(k) = \lambda_{\min} \left(B_j(k) \right) - \left\| K_j(k) \right\|^2 \left\| A_j(k) \right\|^2 - 2 \left\| z_j \left(x_a(k-l), \widehat{x}_b(k), u(k) \right) \right\|^2, \tag{5.49}$$

$$F_j(k) = 1 - \eta_j^2 \left\| C \right\|^2 \left\| K_j(k) \right\|^2 \lambda_{\max} A_j(k) - 2 \left\| C \right\|^2 \left\| g_j \right\|^2 - \eta_j^2 \left\| C \right\|^2, \tag{5.50}$$

inequality (5.48) can be rewritten as

$$\Delta V_j(k) \leq - \left\| \widetilde{w}_j(k) \right\|^2 E_j(k) - \left\| \widetilde{x}(k) \right\|^2 F_j(k) + 2 \left| \epsilon'_{z_j} \right|^2.$$

Hence, $\Delta V_j(k) \leq 0$ whenever

$$\left\| \widetilde{x}(k) \right\|^2 > \sqrt{\frac{2 \left| \epsilon'_{z_j} \right|^2}{F_j(k)}}$$

or

$$\left\| \widetilde{w}_j(k) \right\|^2 > \sqrt{\frac{2 \left| \epsilon'_{z_j} \right|^2}{E_j(k)}}.$$

Therefore, the solution of (5.35) and (5.38) is SGUUB, hence the estimation error and the RONO weights are SGUUB [35].

Now, to finish the proof, consider the following Lyapunov function candidate:

$$V(k) = \sum_{i=1}^{n} \widetilde{w}_i^T(k) P_i(k) \widetilde{w}_i(k) + \widetilde{x}_i(k) \widetilde{x}_i(k), \tag{5.51}$$

$$\Delta V(k) = \sum_{i=1}^{n} \Big(\widetilde{w}_i^T(k+1) P_i(k+1) \widetilde{w}_i(k+1) + \widetilde{x}_i(k+1) \widetilde{x}_i(k+1)$$
$$- \widetilde{w}_i^T(k) P_i(k) \widetilde{w}_i(k) - \widetilde{x}_i(k) \widetilde{x}_i(k) \Big).$$

Therefore, as above, (5.51) can be expressed as

$$\Delta V(k) \leq \sum_{i=1}^{n} \left(- \left\| \widetilde{w}_i(k) \right\|^2 E_i(k) - \left\| \widetilde{x}(k) \right\|^2 F_i(k) + 2 \left| \epsilon'_{z_i} \right|^2 \right)$$

with

$$E_i(k) = \lambda_{\min} \left(B_i(k) \right) - \left\| K_i(k) \right\|^2 \left\| A_i(k) \right\|^2 - 2 \left\| z_i \left(x_a(k-l), \widehat{x}_b(k), u(k) \right) \right\|^2,$$
$$F_i(k) = 1 - \eta_i^2 \left\| C \right\|^2 \left\| K_i(k) \right\|^2 \lambda_{\max} A_i(k) - 2 \left\| C \right\|^2 \left\| g_i \right\|^2 - \eta_i^2 \left\| C \right\|^2.$$

As a result, $\Delta V(k) \leq 0$ whenever

$$\|\widetilde{x}(k)\|^2 > \sqrt{\frac{2\left|\epsilon'_{z_i}\right|^2}{F_i(k)}} \equiv \kappa_1$$

or

$$\|\widetilde{w}_i(k)\|^2 > \sqrt{\frac{2\left|\epsilon'_{z_i}\right|^2}{E_i(k)}} \equiv \kappa_2,$$

and if $\|\widetilde{x}(k)\| > \kappa_1$ or $\|\widetilde{w}_i(k)\| > \kappa_2$, $\forall i = 1, \dots, n$ holds, then $\Delta V(k) \leq 0$.

Finally, from (5.30) it is easy too see that the output error has an algebraic relation with $\widetilde{x}(k)$ and for this reason, if $\widetilde{x}(k)$ is bounded, then $e(k)$ is bounded, too:

$$e(k) = C\widetilde{x}(k),$$
$$\|e(k)\| = \|C\| \|\widetilde{x}(k)\|. \qquad \qquad \Box$$

Considering Theorem 5.2 and its proof, it can be easily shown that the result can be extended to systems with multiple delays like $x(k - l_i)$ with $i = 1, 2, \dots,$ instead of $x(k - l)$ in (5.3) and/or for time-varying delays $x(k - l_i(k))$ with $l_i(k)$ bounded, i.e., when $l_i(k) \leq l$.

5.5 APPLICATIONS

5.5.1 van der Pol System

In this subsection we include the simulation results of the proposed neural observers (full and reducer order) with time-delays, which are implemented online for an oscillator similar to a van der Pol system.

5.5.1.1 Full Order Neural Observer for a van der Pol Oscillator

In order to show the performance of the proposed full order neural observer, the following nonlinear time-delay system is used:

$$\dot{x}_1(t) = x_2(t) + 0.001 x_1(t) u(t),$$
$$\dot{x}_2(t) = \left(1 - x_1^2(t)\right) x_2(t) - x_1(t) + x_3(t) u(t)$$
$$\qquad + 2\cos(x_1(t - 3)),$$
$$\dot{x}_3(t) = x_4(t) + 0.01 x_2(t) x_3(t) \exp(u(t)),$$
$$\dot{x}_4(t) = \left(1 - x_3^2(t)\right) x_4(t) - x_3(t) + \frac{u(t)}{\left(1 + x_2^2(t) x_4^2(t)\right)}$$
$$\qquad + 2\left(x_1^2(t - 3) + x_2^2(t - 3)\right)\sin(x_2(t - 3)),$$

$$y_1(t) = x_1(t) + x_2(t),$$
$$y_2(t) = x_3(t) + x_4(t). \qquad \qquad (5.52)$$

Table 5.1 EKF parameters for RHONO

i	P_i	Q_i	R_i	η_i
1	$1.0 \times 10^3 \times \text{diag}(2)$	$9.7 \times 10^5 \times \text{diag}(2)$	$1.0 \times 10^5 \times \text{diag}(2)$	0.4320
2	$1.0 \times 10^7 \times \text{diag}(4)$	$2.2 \times 10^4 \times \text{diag}(4)$	$1.0 \times 10^4 \times \text{diag}(2)$	-0.2440
3	$1.0 \times 10^5 \times \text{diag}(4)$	$7.17 \times 10^5 \times \text{diag}(4)$	$7.85 \times 10^2 \times \text{diag}(2)$	0.3890
4	$20 \times \text{diag}(4)$	$1.0 \times 10^2 \times \text{diag}(4)$	$1.005 \times 10^3 \times \text{diag}(2)$	-39

System (5.52) is an oscillator similar to a van der Pol system [7]. For system (5.52) the following RHONO (5.53) is proposed:

$$\hat{x}_1(k+1) = w_{11}S(\hat{x}_1(k))$$
$$+ w_{12}S(\hat{x}_1(k))S(\hat{x}_2(k))S(\hat{x}_3(k))S(\hat{x}_4(k))u(k),$$
$$\hat{x}_2(k+1) = w_{21}S(\hat{x}_2(k)) + w_{22}S(\hat{x}_1(k))S(\hat{x}_2(k)) + w_{23}S(\hat{x}_3(k))S(\hat{x}_2(k))$$
$$+ w_{24}S(\hat{x}_1(k))S(\hat{x}_2(k))S(\hat{x}_3(k))S(\hat{x}_4(k))u(k),$$
$$\hat{x}_3(k+1) = w_{31}S(\hat{x}_3(k)) + w_{32}S(\hat{x}_1(k))S(\hat{x}_3(k)) + w_{33}S(\hat{x}_3(k))u(k)$$
$$+ w_{34}S(\hat{x}_1(k))S(\hat{x}_2(k))S(\hat{x}_3(k))S(\hat{x}_4(k))u(k),$$
$$\hat{x}_4(k+1) = w_{41}S(\hat{x}_4(k)) + w_{42}S(\hat{x}_1(k))S(\hat{x}_4(k)) + w_{43}S(\hat{x}_3(k))S(\hat{x}_4(k))$$
$$+ w_{44}S(\hat{x}_1(k))S(\hat{x}_2(k))S(\hat{x}_3(k))S(\hat{x}_4(k))u(k), \tag{5.53}$$

with the values for the EKF training (5.13) as in Table 5.1.

The values for g_i are selected as:

$$g_1 = \begin{pmatrix} 0.1 \\ -0.0460 \end{pmatrix}, \quad g_2 = \begin{pmatrix} 0.9150 \\ -0.0090 \end{pmatrix},$$
$$g_3 = \begin{pmatrix} -0.0251 \\ 0.0600 \end{pmatrix}, \quad g_4 = \begin{pmatrix} -0.0390 \\ 1.1680 \end{pmatrix}. \tag{5.54}$$

Figs. 5.3–5.6 display a comparison between the real x_i and observed $\hat{x}_i$, showing that the RHONN observer state estimation of the states of the time-delay system (5.52) is within a bounded error. It is important to note that the results are obtained without a model of the system or previous knowledge about the delays, bounds, or disturbances.

5.5.1.2 Reduced Order Neural Observer for a van der Pol Oscillator

In order to illustrate the performance of the proposed reduced order neural observer for system (5.52), we consider x_3 and x_4 as measurable variables; therefore, we designed a neural observer for x_1 and x_2 and a neural identifier for x_3 and x_4. The proposed RONO is defined as follows:

$$\hat{x}_1(k+1) = w_{11}S(x_1(k))$$
$$+ w_{12}S(x_1(k))S(x_2(k))S(\hat{x}_3(k))S(\hat{x}_4(k))u(k),$$

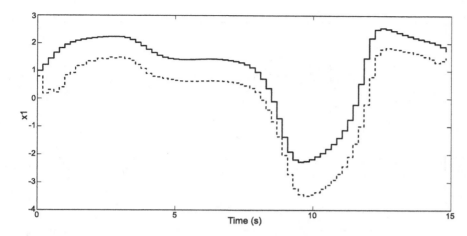

FIGURE 5.3 Real $x_1(k)$ (black solid line) and observed $\hat{x}_1(k)$ (dotted gray line).

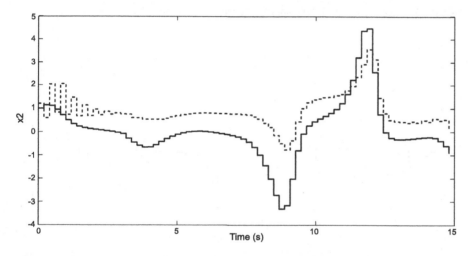

FIGURE 5.4 Real $x_2(k)$ (black solid line) and observed $\hat{x}_2(k)$ (dotted gray line).

$$\hat{x}_2(k+1) = w_{21}S(x_2(k)) + w_{22}S(x_1(k))S(x_2(k)) + w_{23}S(\hat{x}_3(k))S(\hat{x}_2(k))$$
$$+ w_{24}S(x_1(k))S(x_2(k))S(\hat{x}_3(k))S(\hat{x}_4(k))u(k),$$
$$\hat{x}_3(k+1) = w_{31}S(\hat{x}_3(k)) + w_{32}S(x_1(k))S(\hat{x}_3(k)) + w_{33}S(\hat{x}_3(k))u(k)$$
$$+ w_{34}S(x_1(k))S(x_2(k))S(\hat{x}_3(k))S(\hat{x}_4(k))u(k),$$
$$\hat{x}_4(k+1) = w_{41}S(\hat{x}_4(k)) + w_{42}S(x_1(k))S(\hat{x}_4(k)) + w_{43}S(\hat{x}_3(k))S(\hat{x}_4(k))$$
$$+ w_{44}S(x_1(k))S(x_2(k))S(\hat{x}_3(k))S(\hat{x}_4(k))u(k), \tag{5.55}$$

with the values for the EKF training (5.13) as in Table 5.2 and the values for g_i as in (5.54).

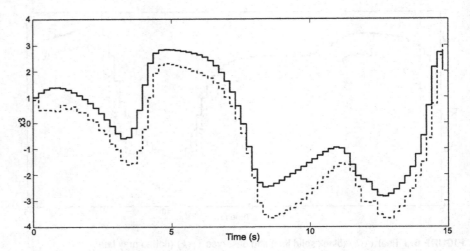

FIGURE 5.5 Real $x_3(k)$ (black solid line) and observed $\hat{x}_3(k)$ (dotted gray line).

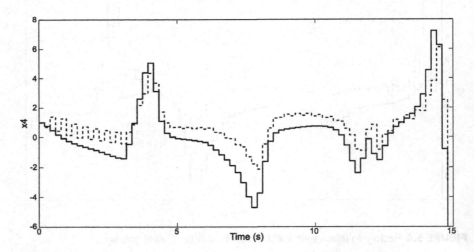

FIGURE 5.6 Real $x_4(k)$ (black solid line) and observed $\hat{x}_4(k)$ (dotted gray line).

Table 5.2 EKF parameters for the RONO

i	P_i	Q_i	R_i	η_i
1	$1.0 \times 10^3 \times \text{diag}(2)$	$9.7 \times 10^5 \times \text{diag}(2)$	$1.0 \times 10^5 \times \text{diag}(2)$	0.4320
2	$1.0 \times 10^7 \times \text{diag}(4)$	$2.2 \times 10^4 \times \text{diag}(4)$	$1.0 \times 10^4 \times \text{diag}(2)$	−0.2440
3	$1.0 \times 10^5 \times \text{diag}(4)$	$7.17 \times 10^5 \times \text{diag}(4)$	$7.85 \times 10^2 \times \text{diag}(2)$	0.3890
4	$20 \times \text{diag}(4)$	$1.0 \times 10^2 \times \text{diag}(4)$	$1.005 \times 10^3 \times \text{diag}(2)$	−39

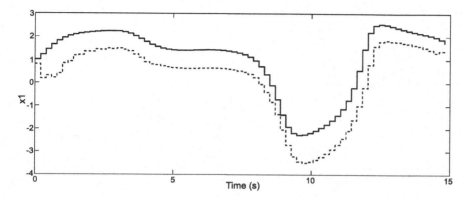

FIGURE 5.7 Real $x_1(k)$ (black solid line) and observed $\hat{x}_1(k)$ (dotted gray line).

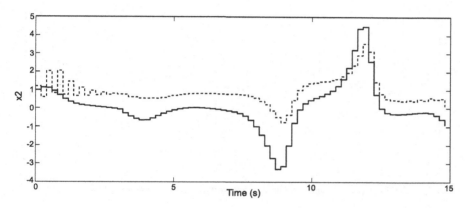

FIGURE 5.8 Real $x_2(k)$ (black solid line) and observed $\hat{x}_2(k)$ (dotted gray line).

Figs. 5.7–5.10 show a comparison between the real x_i and observed $\hat{x}_i$, showing that the RHONN observer state estimation of the states of the time-delay system (5.52) is within a bounded error. It is important to note that the results are obtained without a model of the system or previous knowledge about the delays, bounds, or disturbances.

5.5.2   Linear Induction Motor

In this subsection we include the real time results of the neural observer (full and reducer order) with time-delays, which is implemented online on the same LIM benchmark as explained in Section 3.3.3.3.

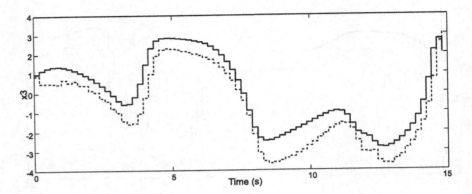

FIGURE 5.9 Real $x_3(k)$ (black solid line) and observed $\hat{x}_3(k)$ (dotted gray line).

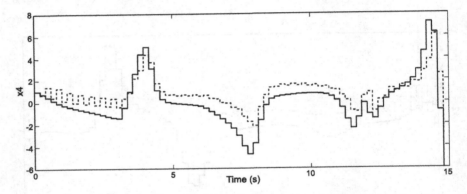

FIGURE 5.10 Real $x_4(k)$ (black solid line) and observed $\hat{x}_4(k)$ (dotted gray line).

5.5.2.1 Full Order Neural Observer for LIM

For the real-time implementation we used a reduced neural observer proposed as follows:

$$\hat{x}_1(k+1) = w_{11}S(\hat{x}_1(k)) + w_{12}\hat{x}_2(k) + g_1 e(k),$$
$$\hat{x}_2(k+1) = w_{21}S(\hat{x}_2(k)) + w_{22}S(\hat{x}_3(k)) + w_{23}S(\hat{x}_4(k)) + w_{24}S(\hat{x}_2(k))S(\hat{x}_4(k))$$
$$+ w_{25}S(\hat{x}_3(k))S(\hat{x}_4(k)) + w_{26}S(\hat{x}_2(k))S(\hat{x}_3(k))$$
$$- w_v S(\hat{x}_3(k)) \sin(n_p \hat{x}_1(k)) + S(\hat{x}_4(k)) \cos(n_p \hat{x}_1(k)))\hat{x}_5(k)$$
$$+ w_v S(\hat{x}_3(k)) \cos(n_p q_m(k-l_1)) - S(\hat{x}_4(k)) \sin(n_p \hat{x}_1(k)))\hat{x}_6(k)$$
$$+ g_2 e(k),$$
$$\hat{x}_3(k+1) = w_{31}S(\hat{x}_2(k)) + w_{32}S(\hat{x}_3(k)) + w_{33}S(\hat{x}_2(k)))S(\hat{x}_3(k))$$
$$+ w_{34}S(\hat{x}_1(k))S(\hat{x}_2(k)) + w_{35}S(\hat{x}_1(k))S(\hat{x}_3(k))$$
$$+ w_{fa} \cos(n_p \hat{x}_1(k))\hat{x}_5(k) + w_{fa} \sin(n_p \hat{x}_1(k))\hat{x}_6(k) + g_3 e(k),$$
$$\hat{x}_4(k+1) = w_{41}S(\hat{x}_2(k)) + w_{42}S(\hat{x}_4(k)) + w_{43}S(\hat{x}_2(k))S(\hat{x}_4(k))$$

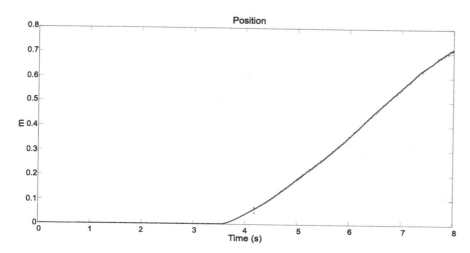

FIGURE 5.11 Real-time position estimation (plant signal (solid line), neural signal (dashed line)).

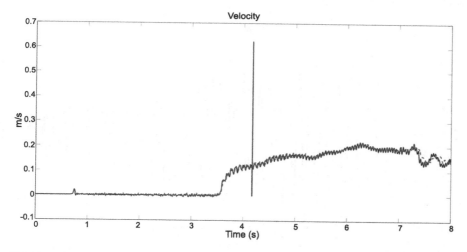

FIGURE 5.12 Real-time velocity estimation (plant signal (solid line), neural signal (dashed line)).

$$+ w_{44} S(\hat{x}_1(k)) S(\hat{x}_2(k)) + w_{45} S(\hat{x}_1(k)) S(\hat{x}_4(k))$$
$$- w_{fa} \sin(n_p \hat{x}_1(k)) \hat{x}_5(k) + w_{fa} \cos(n_p \hat{x}_1(k)) \hat{x}_6(k) + g_4 e(k),$$
$$\hat{x}_5(k+1) = w_{51} S(\hat{x}_2(k)) + w_{52} S(\hat{x}_3(k)) + w_{53} S(\hat{x}_4(k))$$
$$+ w_{54} S(\hat{x}_5(k)) + w_{55} S(\hat{x}_2(k)) S(\hat{x}_3(k)) + w_{56} S(\hat{x}_2(k)) S(\hat{x}_4(k))$$
$$+ w_{57} S(\hat{x}_3(k)) S(\hat{x}_4(k)) + w_{58} u_\alpha(k) + g_5 e(k),$$
$$\hat{x}_6(k+1) = w_{61} S(\hat{x}_2(k)) + w_{62} S(\hat{x}_3(k)) + w_{63} S(\hat{x}_4(k))$$
$$+ w_{64} S(\hat{x}_6(k)) + w_{65} S(\hat{x}_2(k)) S(\hat{x}_3(k)) + w_{66} S(\hat{x}_2(k)) S(\hat{x}_4(k))$$

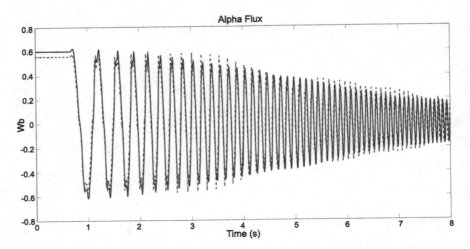

FIGURE 5.13 Real-time alpha flux estimation (plant signal (solid line), neural signal (dashed line)).

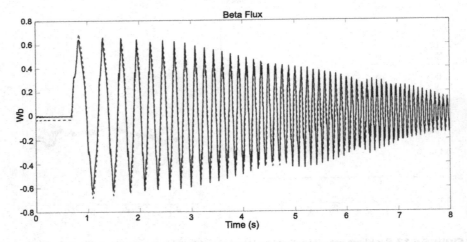

FIGURE 5.14 Real-time beta flux estimation (plant signal (solid line), neural signal (dashed line)).

$$+ w_{67} S(\hat{x}_3(k)) S(\hat{x}_4(k)) + w_{68} u_\beta(k) + g_6 e(k), \tag{5.56}$$

where $S(x(k)) = \alpha \tan h(\beta x(k)) + \gamma$, $\hat{x}_1(k)$ is used to estimate $q_m(k)$, $\hat{x}_2(k)$ to estimate $v(k)$, $\hat{x}_3(k)$ to estimate $\psi_\alpha(k)$, $\hat{x}_4(k)$ to estimate $\psi_\beta(k)$, $\hat{x}_5(k)$ to estimate $i_\alpha(k)$, and $\hat{x}_6(k)$ to estimate $i_\beta(k)$. The input signals u_α and u_β are selected as chirp functions. Both the NN and LIM states are initialized randomly. The associated covariance matrices are initialized as diagonals.

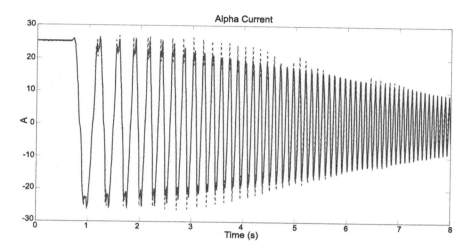

FIGURE 5.15 Real-time alpha current estimation (plant signal (solid line), neural signal (dashed line)).

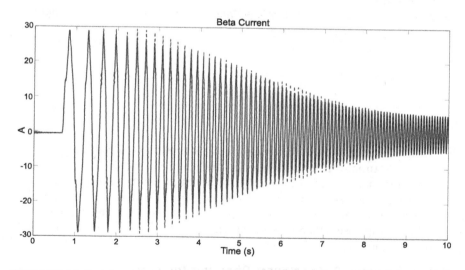

FIGURE 5.16 Real-time beta current estimation (plant signal (solid line), neural signal (dashed line)).

This RONO is implemented online on the same benchmark as explained in Section 3.3.3.3. It is important to remark that the EKF used to develop the RHONN is an online learning algorithm, it is performed using a parallel configuration, and it is computing between samplings. The sampling time is 1 ms.

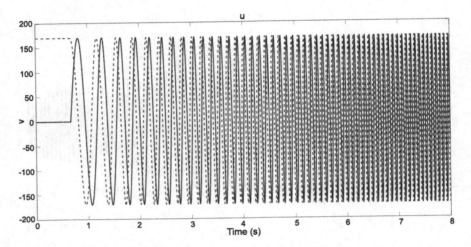

FIGURE 5.17 Applied inputs (alpha voltage (solid line), beta voltage (dashed line)).

Table 5.3 Applied delays

Delay	Signal	Starting Time, in s	Finishing Time, in s	Delay Length, in ms
l_1	q_m	2.9	3.9	3
l_2	v	4.5	5.5	3
l_3	i_α	0	8	3
l_4	i_β	0	8	3

The results of the real-time implementation are presented as follows: Fig. 5.11 displays the estimation performance for the position; Fig. 5.12 presents the velocity performance, Figs. 5.13 and 5.14 present the estimation performance for the fluxes in phase α and β, respectively. Figs. 5.15 and 5.16 portray the estimation performance for currents in phase α and β, respectively; finally, in Fig. 5.17, the input signals are depicted. The applied time-delays are included according to Table 5.3.

5.5.2.2 Reduced Order Neural Observer for LIM
For the real-time implementation we used a reduced neural observer proposed as follows:

$$\hat{x}_1(k+1) = w_{11}S(q_m(k-l_1)) + w_{12}v(k-l_2) + g_1e(k),$$
$$\hat{x}_2(k+1) = w_{21}S(v(k-l_2)) + w_{22}S(\hat{x}_3(k)) + w_{23}S(\hat{x}_4(k))$$
$$+ w_{24}S(v(k-l_2))S(\hat{x}_4(k))$$
$$+ w_{25}S(\hat{x}_3(k))S(\hat{x}_4(k)) + w_{26}S(v(k-l_2))S(\hat{x}_3(k))$$
$$- w_vS(\hat{x}_3(k))\sin(n_pq_m(k-l_1))$$

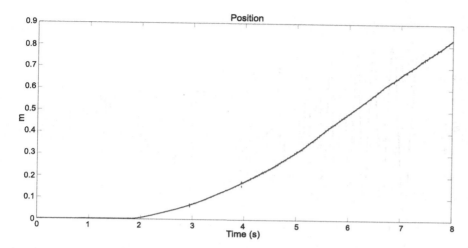

FIGURE 5.18 Real-time position estimation (plant signal (solid line), neural signal (dashed line)).

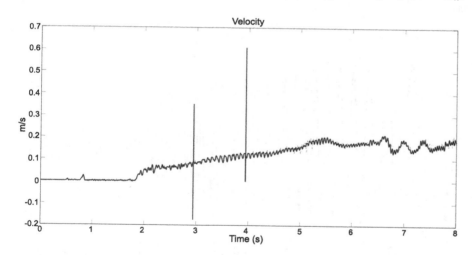

FIGURE 5.19 Real-time velocity estimation (plant signal (solid line), neural signal (dashed line)).

$$
\begin{aligned}
&+ S(\hat{x}_4(k)) \cos(n_p q_m(k - l_1))) i_\alpha(k - l_3) \\
&+ w_v S(\hat{x}_3(k)) \cos(n_p q_m(k - l_1)) \\
&- S(\hat{x}_4(k)) \sin(n_p q_m(k - l_1))) i_\beta(k - l_4) + g_2 e(k), \\
\hat{x}_3(k + 1) =\ & w_{31} S(v(k - l_2)) + w_{32} S(\hat{x}_3(k)) + w_{33} S(v(k - l_2))) S(\hat{x}_3(k)) \\
&+ w_{34} S(q_m(k - l_1)) S(v(k - l_2)) + w_{35} S(q_m(k - l_1)) S(\hat{x}_3(k)) \\
&+ w_{fa} \cos(n_p q_m(k - l_1)) i_\alpha(k - l_3) \\
&+ w_{fa} \sin(n_p q_m(k - l_1)) i_\beta(k - l_4) + g_3 e(k),
\end{aligned}
$$

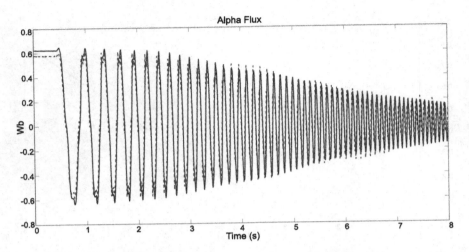

FIGURE 5.20 Real-time alpha flux estimation (plant signal (solid line), neural signal (dashed line)).

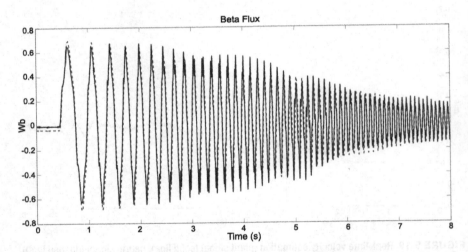

FIGURE 5.21 Real-time beta flux estimation (plant signal (solid line), neural signal (dashed line)).

$$\hat{x}_4(k+1) = w_{41}S(v(k-l_2)) + w_{42}S(\hat{x}_4(k)) + w_{43}S(v(k-l_2))S(\hat{x}_4(k))$$
$$+ w_{44}S(q_m(k-l_1))S(v(k-l_2)) + w_{45}S(q_m(k-l_1))S(\hat{x}_4(k))$$
$$- w_{fa}\sin(n_p q_m(k-l_1))i_\alpha(k-l_3)$$
$$+ w_{fa}\cos(n_p q_m(k-l_1))i_\beta(k-l_4) + g_4 e(k),$$
$$\hat{x}_5(k+1) = w_{51}S(v(k-l_2)) + w_{52}S(\hat{x}_3(k)) + w_{53}S(\hat{x}_4(k))$$
$$+ w_{54}S(i_\alpha(k-l_3))$$

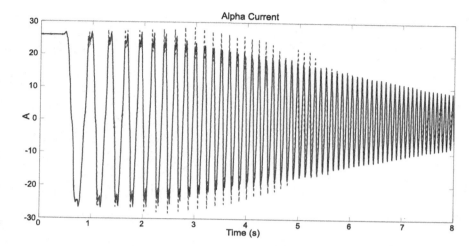

FIGURE 5.22 Real-time alpha current estimation (plant signal (solid line), neural signal (dashed line)).

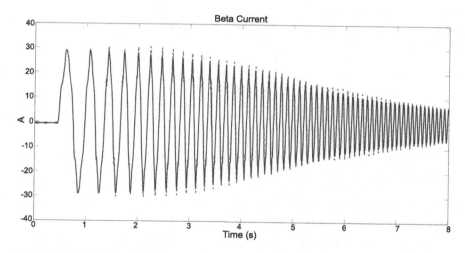

FIGURE 5.23 Real-time beta current estimation (plant signal (solid line), neural signal (dashed line)).

$$
\begin{aligned}
&\quad + w_{55}S(v(k-l_2))S(\hat{x}_3(k)) + w_{56}S(v(k-l_2))S(\hat{x}_4(k)) \\
&\quad + w_{57}S(\hat{x}_3(k))S(\hat{x}_4(k)) + w_{58}u_\alpha(k) + g_5e(k), \\
\hat{x}_6(k+1) &= w_{61}S(v(k-l_2)) + w_{62}S(\hat{x}_3(k)) + w_{63}S(\hat{x}_4(k)) \\
&\quad + w_{64}S(i_\beta(k-l_4)) + w_{65}S(v(k-l_1))S(\hat{x}_3(k)) \\
&\quad + w_{66}S(v(k-l_1))S(\hat{x}_4(k)) \\
&\quad + w_{67}S(\hat{x}_3(k))S(\hat{x}_4(k)) + w_{68}u_\beta(k) + g_6e(k),
\end{aligned}
\tag{5.57}
$$

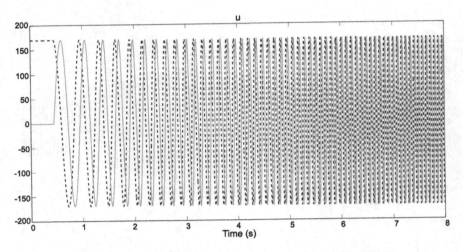

FIGURE 5.24 Applied inputs (alpha voltage (solid line), beta voltage (dashed line)).

Table 5.4 Applied delays

Delay	Starting Time, in s	Finishing Time, in s	Delay Length, in ms
l_1	4.1	4.5	3
l_2	6	8	3
l_3	0	8	3
l_4	0	8	3

where $S(x(k)) = \alpha \tan h(\beta x(k)) + \gamma$, $\hat{x}_1(k)$ is used to estimate $q_m(k)$, $\hat{x}_2(k)$ to estimate $v(k)$, $\hat{x}_3(k)$ to estimate $\psi_\alpha(k)$, $\hat{x}_4(k)$ to estimate $\psi_\beta(k)$, $\hat{x}_5(k)$ to estimate $i_\alpha(k)$, and $\hat{x}_6(k)$ to estimate $i_\beta(k)$. The input signals u_α and u_β are selected as chirp functions. Both the NN and LIM states are initialized randomly. The associated covariance matrices are initialized as diagonals.

This RONO is implemented online on the same benchmark as explained in Section 3.3.3.3. It is important to remark that the EKF used to develop the RHONN is an online learning algorithm, it is performed using a parallel configuration for fluxes and a series–parallel configuration for measurable variables, both of them are computing between samplings. The sampling time is 1 ms.

The results of the real-time implementation are presented as follows: Fig. 5.18 displays the estimation performance for the position; Fig. 5.19 presents the velocity performance, Figs. 5.20 and 5.21 present the estimation performance for the fluxes in phase α and β, respectively. Figs. 5.22 and 5.23 portray the estimation performance for currents in phase α and β, respectively; finally, in

Fig. 5.24, the input signals are depicted. The applied time-delays are included according to Table 5.4.

REFERENCES

[1] E. Boukas, Z. Liu, Deterministic and Stochastic Time Delay Systems, Control Engineering, Birkhäuser, Boston, 2002.

[2] S.S. Ge, K.P. Tee, Adaptive neural network control of nonlinear MIMO time-delay systems with unknown bounds on delay functionals, in: Proceedings of the 2005 American Control Conference, vol. 7, 2005, 2005, pp. 4790–4795.

[3] M. Mahmoud, Robust Control and Filtering for Time Delay Systems, Automation and Control Engineering, Taylor & Francis, 2000.

[4] M. Mahmoud, Switched Time-Delay Systems: Stability and Control, Springer, 2010.

[5] M. Krstic, N. Bekiaris-Liberis, Control of nonlinear delay systems: a tutorial, in: 2012 IEEE 51st Annual Conference on Decision and Control (CDC), 2012, pp. 5200–5214.

[6] Z. Xu, X. Li, Control design based on state observer for nonlinear delay systems, in: 2010 Chinese Control and Decision Conference (CCDC), 2010, pp. 1946–1950.

[7] J. Na, G. Herrmann, X. Ren, P. Barber, Nonlinear observer design for discrete MIMO systems with unknown time delay, in: Proceedings of the 48th IEEE Conference on Decision and Control, 2009 held jointly with the 2009 28th Chinese Control Conference, CDC/CCC 2009, 2009, pp. 6137–6142.

[8] P. Ngoc, Novel criteria for exponential stability of nonlinear differential systems with delay, IEEE Transactions on Automatic Control 60 (2) (2015) 485–490, http://dx.doi.org/10.1109/TAC.2014.2331414.

[9] C. Chen, G.X. Wen, Y.J. Liu, F.Y. Wang, Adaptive consensus control for a class of nonlinear multiagent time-delay systems using neural networks, IEEE Transactions on Neural Networks and Learning Systems 25 (6) (2014) 1217–1226.

[10] H. Xu, S. Jagannathan, Neural network based finite horizon stochastic optimal controller design for nonlinear networked control systems, in: The 2013 International Joint Conference on Neural Networks (IJCNN), 2013, pp. 1–7.

[11] H. Xu, S. Jagannathan, Stochastic optimal controller design for uncertain nonlinear networked control system via neuro dynamic programming, IEEE Transactions on Neural Networks and Learning Systems 24 (3) (2013) 471–484.

[12] J. Kurose, K. Ross, Computer Networking: A Top–Down Approach. Always Learning, Pearson, 2013.

[13] M. Norgaard, Neural Networks for Modelling and Control of Dynamic Systems: A Practitioner's Handbook, Springer, London, 2000.

[14] L. Fu, P. Li, The research survey of system identification method, in: 2013 5th International Conference on Intelligent Human–Machine Systems and Cybernetics (IHMSC), vol. 2, 2013, pp. 397–401.

[15] S. Haykin, Neural Networks: A Comprehensive Foundation, Prentice Hall, 1999.

[16] E. Sanchez, A. Alanis, A. Loukianov, Discrete-Time High Order Neural Control: Trained with Kalman Filtering, Springer, 2008.

[17] M. Hermans, B. Schrauwen, One step Backpropagation Through Time for learning input mapping in reservoir computing applied to speech recognition, in: Proceedings of 2010 IEEE International Symposium on Circuits and Systems (ISCAS), 2010, pp. 521–524.

[18] Y. Bengio, P. Simard, P. Frasconi, Learning long-term dependencies with gradient descent is difficult, IEEE Transactions on Neural Networks 5 (2) (1994) 157–166.

[19] S. Hochreiter, Recurrent neural net learning and vanishing gradient, International Journal of Uncertainty, Fuzziness and Knowledge-Based Systems 6 (2) (1998) 107–116.

[20] S. Haykin, Kalman Filtering and Neural Networks, Wiley, 2004.

[21] Y. Zhang, V. Sircoulomb, N. Langlois, Observer design for discrete-time systems subject to long time-delay, in: 2012 24th Chinese Control and Decision Conference (CCDC), 2012, pp. 2949–2954.

[22] P. Chang, J.W. Lee, Time delay observer: a robust observer for nonlinear plants using time-delayed signals, in: Proceedings of the 1995 American Control Conference, vol. 3, 1995, pp. 1638–1642.

[23] P. Chang, S. Park, The enhanced time delay observer for nonlinear systems, in: 1998 Proceedings of the 37th IEEE Conference on Decision and Control, vol. 1, 1998, pp. 367–368.

[24] G. Lu, D. Ho, Robust $\mathcal{H}_\infty$ observer for nonlinear discrete systems with time delay and parameter uncertainties, IEEE Proceedings – Control Theory and Applications 151 (4) (2004) 439–444.

[25] T. Raff, F. Allgower, An EKF-based observer for nonlinear time-delay systems, in: 2006 American Control Conference, 2006, p. 4.

[26] Y. Wen, X. Ren, Robust adaptive control based on neural state observer for nonlinear time-delay systems, in: IEEE International Conference on Control and Automation, 2009, ICCA 2009, 2009, pp. 1178–1183.

[27] W. Ruliang, J. Huiying, Observer-based adaptive neural network robust control of nonlinear time-delay systems with unmodeled dynamics, in: 2010 International Conference on Computational Intelligence and Security (CIS), 2010, pp. 506–510.

[28] S. Yi, Time-Delay Systems: Analysis and Control Using the Lambert W Function, World Scientific, 2010.

[29] Q. Zhong, Robust Control of Time-Delay Systems, Springer, 2006.

[30] Jean-Pierre Richard, Time-delay systems: an overview of some recent advances and open problems, Automatica 39 (2003) 1667–1694.

[31] T. Xian-Ming, Y. Jin-Shou, Stability analysis for discrete time-delay systems, in: Fourth International Conference on Networked Computing and Advanced Information Management, vol. 1, 2008, NCM '08, 2008, pp. 648–651.

[32] A.Y. Alanis, J.D. Rios, N. Arana Daniel, C. Lopez Franco, Neural identifier for unknown discrete-time nonlinear delayed systems, Neural Computing and Applications (2015) 1–12.

[33] Y. Song, J. Grizzle, The extended Kalman filter as a local asymptotic observer for nonlinear discrete-time systems, in: 1992 American Control Conference, 1992, pp. 3365–3369.

[34] J. Sarangapani, Neural Network Control of Nonlinear Discrete-Time Systems, CRC Press, Taylor & Francis Group, Boca Raton, FL, USA, 2006.

[35] Y.H. Kim, F.L. Lewis, High-Level Feedback Control with Neural Networks, World Scientific, Singapore, 1998.

CHAPTER 6

Final Remarks

ABSTRACT

This chapter states relevant conclusions and future trends about discrete-time neural observers, their analysis and applications.

CONTENTS

KEYWORDS

Full order observers

Reduced order observers

Neural observers

Unknown discrete-time nonlinear systems

Unknown discrete-time delayed nonlinear systems

6.1 FINAL REMARKS

The intention of this chapter is to establish a book summary with some final remarks, conclusions, and future work. In this book, the authors discussed the application of RHONN trained with an EKF-based algorithm for state estimation of unknown discrete-time nonlinear systems; under the presence of external and internal disturbances, and delays without the previous knowledge of their dynamics, measurements, bounds, or explicit estimation. Even if all these conditions appear exaggerated, they are present more than expected, mainly in real-life systems. Such conditions provoke failures of traditional control strategies; therefore, the applicability of the proposed neural observers is large, as has been illustrated trough this book with different applications including HIV, anaerobic systems for wastewater treatment, electromechanical systems (rotatory and linear induction motors), and oscillators like that of van der Pol. All these applications, of very different nature, exemplify the power of the proposed neural observers.

In Chapter 1, a brief motivation of this book is included along with the problem statement, book structure, and used notation. This chapter also judges the importance of autonomous systems and the reason to consider neural net-

Discrete-Time Neural Observers. DOI: 10.1016/B978-0-12-810543-6.00006-X

works as a useful tool to implement observers for unknown discrete nonlinear systems.

Chapter 2 includes mathematical preliminaries, like stability definitions for discrete-time nonlinear systems, a brief introduction to artificial neural networks, particularly to discrete-time high order ones, trained with an EKF based algorithm, and the importance of nonlinear observers mainly for modern control theory.

In order to begin treating neural observers of this book, Chapter 3 proposes the design of full order neural observers for unknown discrete-time nonlinear systems considering linear and nonlinear output cases, such observers are designed based on an RHONN trained with an EKF to simultaneously estimate the plant dynamics (plant model) and the state variables' measurement only with output measurements.

Then in order to reduce computational complexity, in Chapter 4, we proposed the use of available measurements to develop the neural observer only for unmeasurable variables and to estimate the dynamics of the measurable ones using a neural identifier. Finally, in Chapter 5, these results are reconsidered for discrete-time unknown nonlinear systems with delays, expanding the possible applications of the proposed neural observers.

All these results allow obtaining accurate mathematical models and state estimations for a wide class of unknown nonlinear systems to be analyzed, controlled, predicted, simulated, emulated, etc. The applications considered in this book include experimental and simulation results showing once more the importance and capabilities of the proposed observers. It is important to remark that all the proposed neural observers are complemented with the respective stability proof, ensuring the weight estimation error, the output error, and the state estimation error bounds in the presence of bounded disturbances.

Finally, we emphasize the highlights of the book:

- This book contributes to establishing this analysis for discrete-time unknown nonlinear state estimation.
- In order to guarantee error boundedness, an EKF learning algorithm is proposed for online weight estimation of RHONN.
- The proposed neural schemes are very general in the sense that they are able to handle a large class of discrete-time nonlinear systems.
- The proposed observers allow simultaneously estimating the unmeasurable variables and the system model.
- The proposed observers deal with discrete-time unknown nonlinear systems with linear or nonlinear output and with or without delays.
- The proposed observers allow designing full or reduced order observers for discrete-time unknown nonlinear systems. Due the online adaptability of the proposed observers, they can be implemented in real-time implementations for real-life systems.

In regards to future work and maybe as a source for inspiration, the following future work is suggested:

- Constructing neural observers for unknown discrete-time nonlinear systems with stochastic delays;
- Obtaining neural observers for unknown discrete-time nonlinear systems with packet looses;
- Establishing neural observers for unknown stochastic discrete-time nonlinear systems;
- Constructing neuro-evolvable observers for unknown discrete-time nonlinear systems;
- Providing their applications to different real-life systems; and
- Illustrating their application to control different real-life systems.

Finally, we are sure that this book will help the new generation of students and scientists to apply the ideas proposed in this book in their research activities, both theoretical and practical.

Index

133

Printed in the United States
By Bookmasters